D0501130

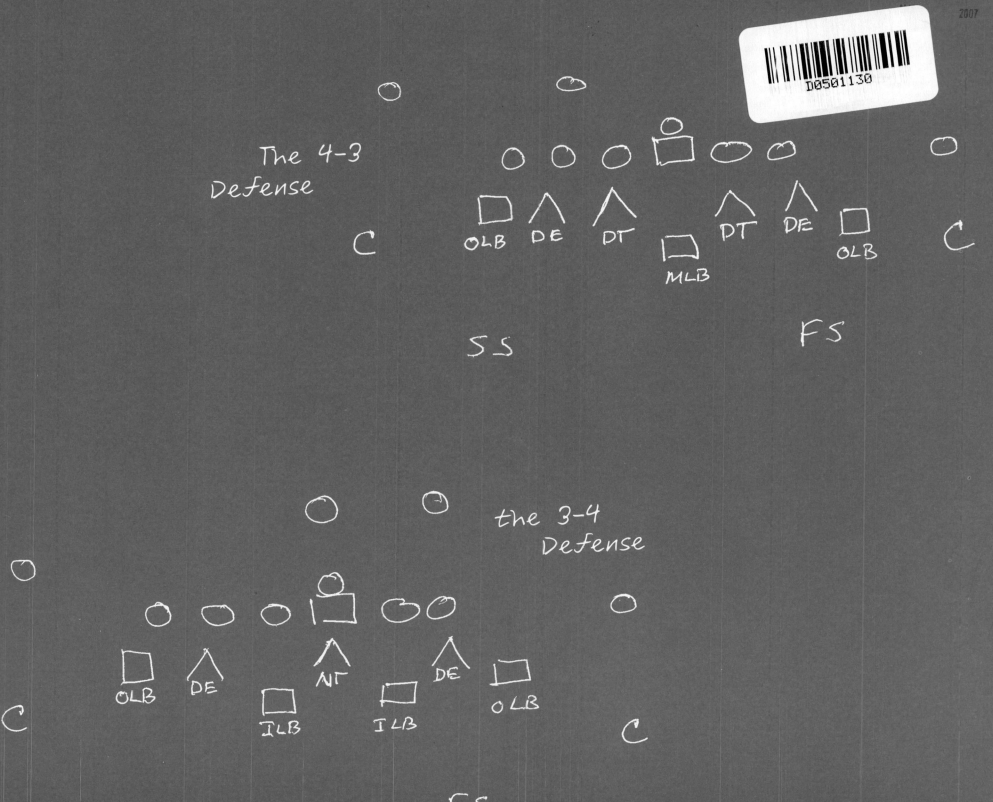

The 4-3
Defense

OLB DE DT DT DE OLB

MLB

C   C

SS   FS

the 3-4
Defense

OLB DE NT DE OLB

ILB ILB

C   C

SS   FS

MONTEREY PUBLIC LIBRARY

JOHN MADDEN'S
HEROES OF FOOTBALL
THE STORY OF AMERICA'S GAME

with Bill Gutman

Dutton Children's Books

J
796
MAD

This book is dedicated to my grandchildren:
Jack, Jesse, Sam, Aidan, and Makenna —J.M.

Photo Credits: Al Messerschmidt/WireImage.com: pp 54, 59, 60, 63, 64, 66, 67, 68, 70, 72, 74; Al Pereira/WireImage.com: p. 76; Allen Kee/WireImage.com: pp. 73, 75 (top); Arthur Anderson/WireImage.com: p. 56; Courtesy of John Madden (photographed by Patrick Simone): p. 5; Frank Rippon/WireImage.com: pp. 29, 31; Fred Roe/WireImage.com: p. 53; George Gellatly/WireImage.com: p. 35; James Flores/WireImage.com: pp. 47, 48; Manny Rubio/WireImage.com: p. 62; Mike Erhmann/WireImage.com: p. 75 (bottom); NFL/WireImage.com: pp. 15, 37, 46, 52 (top), 55, 77 (top); Notre Dame University/WireImage.com: p. 11; Pro Football Hall of Fame/WireImage.com: pp. 8, 10, 12, 16, 18, 19, 21, 22, 24, 26, 27, 28, 30, 36; Rod Hanna/WireImage.com: p. 50; Takashi Makita/WireImage.com: p. 52 (bottom); The Cleveland Browns: p. 32; The Yale University Athletics Department Archives: p. 6; Tom Hauck/WireImage.com: p. 76 (bottom); University Archives, California Polytechnic State University, San Luis Obispo: p. 4; Vernon Biever/WireImage.com: pp. 17, 40, 41, 43, 45, 49, 57; Vic Stein/WireImage.com: p. 34

Text copyright © 2006 by Red Bear, Inc.
Copyright © 2006 by Red Bear, Inc. &
Byron Preiss Visual Publications, Inc.
All rights reserved.

LIBRARY OF CONGRESS CATALOGING-IN-PUBLICATION DATA
Madden, John.
    John Madden's heroes of football : the story of america's game/by John Madden with Bill Gutman.
        p. cm.
    Includes bibliographical references and index.
    ISBN 0-525-47698-9
    1. Football players—United States—Biography—Juvenile literature. 2. Football—History—Juvenile literature. I. Gutman, Bill. II. Title.
    GV939.A1M33 2006
    796.332092'2—dc22   2005036019

Published in the United States by Dutton Children's Books,
a division of Penguin Young Readers Group
345 Hudson Street, New York, New York 10014
www.penguin.com/youngreaders

Designed by Nathan Savage / Red Herring Design

Manufactured in China • First Edition
10 9 8 7 6 5 4 3 2 1

CONTENTS

Introduction

Growing up near San Francisco in Daly City, California, I started playing football when I was about eight or nine years old. In those days there was no television, no videos, and no video games, so we just used our imaginations. There was an empty lot alongside our house and, while my family didn't own it, everyone called it Madden's Lot. We used to play there every day until someone decided to build a house on it.

We always organized games ourselves. Sometimes we didn't even have a real ball, but we'd still play. We'd stuff some rags into a paper bag, and just like that we had a *football*. Like I said, we used our imaginations and we improvised. When you have to create your own field, set the boundaries (maybe a tree on one side and an old sweatshirt dropped on the ground for the other), and make the rules, it somehow becomes more meaningful. Because of all these diverse elements I probably learned more about what sports should be at Madden's Lot than anywhere else.

As a kid back then, we all played whatever sport was in season. That meant baseball in the spring and summer, football in the fall, and basketball during the winter months. I always loved sports and loved competing, and since everyone moved with the seasons, so did I. Because we never had twenty-two guys to make up a full eleven-to-a-side team during football season, we would create a game for whatever number of players we had. We even played one-on-one if there were only two of us. Sometimes it was two-on-two or four-on-four. If we only had a very small area, we'd even play on our knees and tackle that way. So no matter where we were or how many guys we had, we could always play football.

As a lineman for California Polytechnic, John wore number 74. These caricatures of the players are from a team guide.

When I was young, the only way to "watch" football was to listen to it on the radio. I went to my first college game when I was about ten years old—the University of San Francisco against Wyoming at Kezar Stadium in San Francisco. The college game was much more prominent than the pros back then. The 49ers arrived in 1946 with the old All-American Football Conference and finally joined the NFL in 1950. But to us, college All-Americans were bigger heroes than the pros. These were the guys we wanted to imitate. There was a running back at St. Mary's, Herman Wedemeyer, who used to jump over tacklers. I remember telling one of my friends to get down low and I'd be Herman Wedemeyer and try to jump over him.

Finally, I began going to see the 49ers. They had a great tackle named Bob Toneff, who wore number 74. He was my favorite, and whatever I played after watching him, I always wanted to be number 74. Sometimes we would sneak into a preseason game because we couldn't afford a ticket. At the end of these preseason games you could go down on the field and walk off with the players. I always liked to stand next to them just to see how big they were and to check out their equipment close up. We also went to see the 49ers train at St. Mary's College in Moraga, which was about twenty miles east of San Francisco. In those days very few people were there, maybe a couple of writers and about ten or fifteen fans. So you could stand on the sidelines watching the players and listening to the coaches. That was another way to learn.

In high school, I grew quite a bit and knew I would be a lineman. As a young kid, you don't know what position you'll wind up playing. Most kids want to be a quarterback, running back, or wide receiver.

They never think about being a lineman. That's something you kind of grow into naturally. In fact, football is kind of a tough sport to be really good at before you get to high school. Until then, you should just play the game and enjoy it. If you're going to wind up being an offensive or defensive lineman, a linebacker or a tight end, you'll know it in time.

In my junior year, the Philadelphia Eagles drafted me. In those days they could draft you as a junior and then you returned to play as a senior. That's when I decided to be a professional football player and finally gave up baseball. Then I hurt my knee during my first training camp with the Eagles. I used to come in before practice to get treatment, and I would always find Eagles quarterback Norm Van Brocklin there already, watching game films. He eventually asked me to come sit with him, and I'd listen to his comments. He was talking to himself through me, and I learned more football than ever before. Van Brocklin was a bright guy, and he taught me all about the passing game and how to attack a defense. Once I learned my knee injury was so bad that I could no longer play, I was ready to go into coaching. Sports were something I had done all my life, and I wasn't ready to give them up and wear a suit and tie every day.

Some people still ask me, why football? After all, I loved all sports as a kid. However, with football you're competing in a true team sport. Sure, baseball is also a team sport, but there are also many individual confrontations—the pitcher and the batter, the catcher and the guy trying to steal a base, the outfielder trying to throw out a base runner—things like that. Football is different. It is always the *team*. If you do your job but someone else doesn't, the team won't be successful. You know you have to put it all together, especially on offense. If just one person doesn't do the right thing, the entire play can break down

and not work. You always have to rely on one another. So it is the competition, the team, and also the physical part of it. Hit and be hit. At some point that has to be enjoyable to you, or you'll eventually stop playing.

The following pages will tell you all about the sport that still means so much to me after all these years—professional football. Along the way you'll find out about the growth of the game, the many rule changes, the great teams, and the outstanding players who have been running onto professional football fields for many, many years. As with other sports, it's the players who make the game. Many of the top players were trailblazers, showing their finely honed skills both to the fans and to those players who came after and would take the game to the next level. These special players often had the combination of talent, style, and personality—qualities that made fans want to come out and see them in action. Without them, the game could not have grown and developed the way it has.

Football is also a uniquely American game, its top players becoming American sports legends. The growth of television has gone hand in hand with the growth of the game in the second half of the twentieth century. Because the sport plays so well on the tube, it gives everyone the chance to watch their favorite players in action week after week during the season. This book will give you an opportunity to learn about the complete history of professional football and how it has evolved into the great sport that it is today. By learning about the game, you'll also have a better idea why your favorite players today are so special and exciting, and why they are continuing a tradition that began more than a hundred years ago.

Enjoy.

As a rookie with the Philadelphia Eagles in 1958, John saw a possible pro career ended by a knee injury. From there it was on to coaching.

CHAPTER 1

The 1879 Yale University football team. The Elis were captained by Walter Camp, who would become known as the Father of American Football.

The Beginnings

to 1920

From the very beginning, football was a rough-and-tumble game. The sport evolved from a variety of crude and unorganized games in which a ball was kicked or pushed, grabbed, and jumped on. Games like this were played in many countries even before America was settled. When more and more people began coming to the original thirteen colonies from England, a form of football arrived along with them. Players would use a pig's bladder as a ball while pushing against each other to try to advance. There were many different versions with different sets of rules. Some even called the game "football."

However, the game that would evolve into modern American football began in earnest at three of the Ivy League colleges in the East (Harvard, Yale, Princeton) as class competition. The incoming freshmen would play against returning sophomores. The game partially resembled the English sport of rugby, and it was rough stuff. By the 1840s, players at Yale devised the "flying wedge"—a V-shaped group of blockers who would run interference for the guy with the ball.

The first recorded intercollegiate football game was played on November 6, 1869, only four years after the end of the Civil War. Rutgers and Princeton played each other with twenty-five players on a side and with a black rubber ball that could be kicked or butted with the shoulders. That game, however, was closer to soccer than real football. By 1875, Harvard and Yale played a type of game that used variations of rugby rules and, a year later, four Ivy League schools formed the Intercollegiate Football Association. The game then was still a mix of rugby and soccer rules. Believe me, it was a wild game with little organization.

Soon, rugby was proving more popular than soccer, which probably explains why the game evolved as it did. Rugby was the rougher game with far more body contact. The first real rules for American football were written in 1876. This early game was extremely physical, a game for only very tough men. The early field was long and wide, about 140 by 70 yards, compared to today's field, which is 120 yards long (including two 10-yard end zones) and 53 ⅓ yards wide, and the players wore no headgear or other protective padding. It was even said that some players allowed their hair to grow very long to give them a little extra protection when they bumped heads. So long hair goes way back, and no one objected then. But the game was still more like mass confusion than a well-defined sport. There wasn't tackling as we know it, just a lot of shoving, pushing, punching, and gouging. Serious injuries were frequent. It was a rough, rough game, but there are some tough modern players who probably would have enjoyed it.

A Yale undergraduate named Walter Camp would have the biggest early influence on the game. In fact, he would become known as the Father of American Football. Camp was a driving force in getting the number of players reduced from fifteen to eleven on a side in 1880, as well as having the size of the field reduced to 110 yards long by 53 yards wide. In addition, Camp is given credit for creating the line of scrimmage and allowing the center to snap the ball to a player in the backfield to start a play. By starting plays in this way, the offensive team could begin to plan their plays in advance. Just these few innovations alone made a game of mass confusion begin to look more like modern-day football.

By 1882, the rules committee, again led by Walter Camp, made a change that would require a team to gain five yards on three downs in order to keep possession of the ball. To measure more accurately, Camp said the field would have to be marked with chalk lines every five yards. Over the next few years he and the rules committee began to refine the scoring process. At one point, a touchdown was two points and a field goal five. Then it was modified to four for a TD; two points for a conversion, kicking the ball through the uprights after a score; and two points for a safety, when an offensive player with the ball is tackled behind his own goal line. Today, of course, a touchdown counts six points and a field goal three, but slowly football was starting to look like football. Some of the old rules are hard to believe now. Imagine how today's game would look if a touchdown was just two points and a field goal five? What would be the sense trying to score a TD when you could just kick it through the uprights?

The First Pros Arrive

William "Pudge" Heffelfinger is widely considered the first professional football player, or at least the first to admit he took money for his services. Heffelfinger was a guard at Yale, a fine player who was part of Walter Camp's very first All-America team in 1889. He graduated in 1891 and a year later was offered the then-handsome sum of $500 to play for the Allegheny Athletic Association in a game against the Pittsburgh Athletic Club. Their money was well spent. Pudge picked up a fumble and ran for the only score of the game, which Allegheny won 4-0.

A year later, the Greensburg Athletic Association, also in Pennsylvania, decided they wanted a top player, too. The guy they wanted was Lawson Fiscus, who had been a halfback at Princeton. Fiscus was given $20 a game plus expenses. Today, that same amount

Yale graduate Pudge Heffelfinger is widely considered the first professional football player.

of money wouldn't even purchase ten gallons of gas, but back then it made Fiscus a professional, a guy who was making money playing a game he loved. Soon more players were beginning to play for local athletic clubs and being paid to do it. Some received as little as $10 a game, but it was still play-for-pay, and that made them pros. At the same time, the game continued to change and move slowly toward resembling modern-day football.

Blocking was soon changed to eliminate the use of the hands and extending the arms. While there were already four players in the backfield—a quarterback, two halfbacks, and a fullback—there was no real passing. The quarterback might flip or lateral the ball to a running back, but the ball used back then was fat in the middle, almost round, and extremely difficult to pass. The players, however, already lined up in the backfield in a way that resembled the straight-T formation.

Very few players wore padding then. A few running backs wore small skullcaps, but Heffelfinger, for one, thought any kind of headgear just wasn't his kind of football.

"None of that sissy stuff for me," he once purportedly said. "I just let my hair grow long and pull it through my turtleneck sweater." That's the kind of tough game football was then.

The first team to use headgear full time was the Carlisle Indian School college team. Their coach, Glenn "Pop" Warner, mandated headgear for all his players in 1897. By that time there were more professional teams, but even the teams that began to pay all their players often just had games on weekends because the players had to

THE NESSERS, A FOOTBALL FAMILY

Not all the early professional football players came from the college ranks. In the early days, the first family of pro football had to be the Nessers of Columbus, Ohio. Both father and sons became boilermakers who were employed by the Panhandle Division of the Pennsylvania Railroad. That was their job. Their lives were football. The family members were immigrants from Alsace, France, who came to America around the turn of the century. None of the boys went to college, but they all played football and played it well.

John Nesser was a quarterback while brother Phil was a fine all-around athlete, good enough to get college scholarships if that had been his choice. Frank could punt the ball from one end of the field to the other, while Al was a forward passer and a vicious defender who would take on any blocker or running back. Ted Jr. was the fifth member of the football-playing brothers. If you look at the photograph of the Columbus Panhandles from 1911, six Nessers are staring at the camera, including Ted Jr.'s son, Fred, all with grim, determined faces. Al played the longest, into his forties, and never wore so much as an athletic supporter. Now that's tough! Yet in later years, looking back at the game he and his family loved, he said, "Football was made for everybody to enjoy."

earn a real living during the week. The $10 or so they received to play football was extra money, a part-time job. There were some attempts to form leagues in the early years of the twentieth century, but none really stabilized. Pro football was still a sport in its infancy.

Perhaps the strongest early pro league was in Ohio, where the team from the city of Massillon won the championship in 1904. Massillon was located just west of Canton, and the two cities would produce teams that would be archrivals for years. At the time, the winner of the Ohio League was considered the professional champion. Because the league had quickly become popular, there was talk about expanding to more teams, giving players larger salaries, and writing standard rules for the game. That year, a halfback named Charles Follis signed with the Shelby (Ohio) Athletic Club and became the first known African-American professional football player.

The next year, Massillon won again and the Canton (Ohio) AC joined the league. The Canton team would soon become known as the Bulldogs. A year after that the forward pass became legal with the first-ever pass completion in a pro game coming on October 27, 1906, when George "Peggy" Parratt of Massillon threw to teammate Dan "Bullet" Riley in a win against a combined Benwood-Moundsville team. If nothing else, the players had some wild nicknames in those days. As with almost every rule change down through the years, the result was to make the game better and to make the offense more effective. That would hold true all the way to modern times.

Jim Thorpe Helps Put Pro Football on the Map

Professional football was still undergoing growing pains in the first two decades of the twentieth century. There was a crisis in 1905 when President Theodore Roosevelt, himself an avid sportsman, felt football was producing too many serious injuries. Images of bloodied players being led from the field angered the president, and he demanded reforms or threatened to abolish the game. Hard to believe that a game like football could be *too* rough, but even Walter Camp agreed. He replied to President Roosevelt's request by saying, in part:

"Unless steps are taken to reform the sport, we shall discover that our precious football is being relegated to the ash heap of history.

Jim Thorpe, shown here dropkicking the ball, was football's first superstar and one of the greatest all-around athletes ever.

Brutality has no place in this sport. This is a game that must train its followers, its players, and its spectators in the qualities of successful character."

One of the rule changes that made the sport a little less violent was the creation of a "neutral zone" on the line of scrimmage in 1906. Before that, linemen had a tendency to begin hitting each other before the ball was even snapped. Talk about a game being out of control! Now, players had to stay out of the neutral zone until the ball was snapped. Otherwise, they were declared *offsides*, leading to a penalty, a rule that is still enforced today.

By 1910, the rules committee gave the offensive team four downs, or plays, to make a first down, which allowed the offensive team to keep the ball for another four downs, and that further encouraged the use of the pass. The college game was still thriving, and the hotbed of the professional game continued to be Ohio. The Massillon and Canton rivalry had been slowed by a gambling scandal, but other Ohio teams were becoming more popular. And a player was about to come along who would become professional football's first superstar and well-known personality. And he came along just at the right time.

His name was Jim Thorpe. He was part Sac and Fox Native American and born on May 28, 1888, near Prague, Oklahoma. Jim grew up in an open area of Oklahoma, where he loved to run and jump and would often do it for hours on end. He was finally sent to the Carlisle Indian School in Carlisle, Pennsylvania, to pursue a college education. Once there he began participating in track, where he was an immediate star, and eventually went out for the football team, coached by the legendary Glenn "Pop" Warner. Thorpe quickly became a superstar in both sports. On the football field he was a great broken-field runner on offense and a tenacious defender who hit as hard as anyone. In addition, he could punt and dropkick with the best of them. It wouldn't be long before his coach would call him "the greatest football player of all time."

Jim Thorpe was an All-American in both the 1911 and 1912 seasons. The All-American team honored the best college players in the land and was chosen annually by Walter Camp, who began the tradition in 1889. During his two All-American seasons, Jim Thorpe had many great games. Among them was a 1911 upset of an outstanding Harvard team in which Jim ran for a 70-yard touchdown and dropkicked four field goals. A year later he scored twenty-two points all by himself as Carlisle upset mighty Army 27-6. He wound up his senior year with twenty-five touchdowns and 198 points. Earlier that summer, Jim had traveled to Stockholm, Sweden, where he won both the pentathlon and decathlon at the Olympic Games, something no other athlete has ever done. He would later have his Olympic medals taken from him because he had been paid to play semipro baseball in the summer of 1909. But they were finally returned to his family in 1982, something that was long overdue.

But it was football where Jim would ultimately make his mark. He was an assistant coach at Indiana University for two years and even played Major League Baseball with the New York Giants, but toward the end of the 1915 season he signed with football's Canton Bulldogs. Most pros were getting between $75 and $100 per game, but Jim was offered $250 a game to help rebuild the franchise. Thanks to Thorpe, the Canton-Massillon rivalry was revived, and the

games were often epic battles with huge crowds for the day of 8,000 or more fans lining the field.

In the final game of the 1915 season, Thorpe was said to have been stopped on his first run by Knute Rockne, who was already an assistant coach at Notre Dame but still playing end for Massillon. When he stopped him again, Thorpe got mad. On his third carry he ripped right over Rockne on his way to a long gain. A year later, Thorpe led Canton to the "Championship of the World" as the Bulldogs beat Massillon 24-0, in the final game for the title. Though the pro game would become less prominent the next two years as the United States became involved in World War I, a new era was soon coming, and the aging Jim Thorpe would still play a major role.

But in his early days with Canton he was something to behold. Most players then were much smaller than their counterparts today, but those who saw Jim Thorpe and also lived long enough to see players of the modern era always felt that the great Native American would have transcended his time. Many of the great ones can do that. Not only was he a great football player, but he was one of the greatest athletes who ever lived, an extremely physical man who always gave back more punishment than he received on the field, something many feel he would have done no matter what era he played in. No doubt about it, Jim Thorpe was the greatest professional player of the first two decades of the twentieth century.

Knute Rockne, shown in his old uniform in 1930, played and later coached at Notre Dame and is still considered an outstanding coach and top football strategist.

CHAPTER 2

Green Bay Packers head coach "Curly" Lambeau diagrams a play for quarterback Cecil Isbell (center) and Hall of Fame end Don Hutson in 1940.

The Early Days of the National Football League

1920-1933

By 1919, professional football was growing in popularity, but it was pretty much an unorganized mess and there were a number of unrelated leagues. That year, Canton again won the Ohio League championship, and joining the Ohio League for the first time were the Green Bay Packers. Earl "Curly" Lambeau and George Calhoun organized the new team, while Lambeau's boss at the Indian [meat] Packing Company forked over $500 for equipment and also gave the team the use of the company field for practice. Thus the name Packers. Who would think today that a football team would be named for a meat-packing plant, or that the name would stick? The Packers went 10-1 in their initial season, but the creation of a stable league still had not happened.

There were three big problems. Salaries were beginning to rise and players were jumping from team to team, looking for and taking the highest offers. Some teams were using college players who were still in school, a practice that was frowned upon since amateur athletes could not be paid. And because there were several pro leagues, the rules often varied, leading to more confusion. Team owners began getting behind the idea of forming a single professional league. After all, Major League Baseball had done it years earlier and was successful. So it made good sense.

The result was a ten-team league originally called the American Professional Football Conference. Four more teams were added during the 1920 season, and the name was changed even before that first year ended to the American Professional Football Association (APFA). But all of the teams were lumped into a single division and did not even play the same number of games. The first game with an APFA team was played on September 26, 1920, when the Rock Island (Illinois) Independents met the non-league St. Paul (Minnesota)

Ideals before a crowd of eight hundred fans at Rock Island's Douglas Park. Rock Island won, 48-0. A week later, the first two APFA teams played at Triangle Park in Dayton. In what is now considered the first real NFL game, the home team, the Dayton Triangles, defeated Columbus with Lou Parlow of Dayton scoring the first touchdown. Basically, that's how it all started, without a lot of excitement except for those who were there. But it was still difficult to see what the future would bring.

During the early 1920s, teams came and went with the numbers changing each year. At the end of each season the team with the best

THE OORANG INDIANS

Perhaps the strangest franchise in the history of professional sports was organized by one of football's greatest players. In 1922, the legendary Jim Thorpe helped form a team that was supposed to consist of all Native American players. The franchise was located in Marion, Ohio, and called the Oorang Indians. Two of Thorpe's Carlisle college teammates, Joe Guyon and Pete Calac, were also on the club. But there weren't enough Native Americans to fill the roster and many players were made "honorary Indians," with names like Eagle Feather, Running Deer, and Tomahawk, but they weren't Native Americans. The team was 3-6 in 1922 and then 1-10 the following season before disbanding. While many people thought their name was that of a Native American tribe, the team was actually named for its sponsor, the Oorang Dog Kennels. That one is really hard to believe.

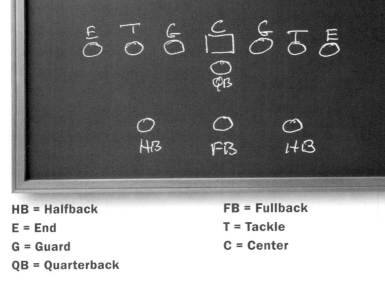

THE BASIC OR TIGHT "T"

The Chicago Bears of the 1940s were the first team to perfect the use of the Basic or Tight "T" formation. The T formation was popular in the 1940s, '50s, and '60s. Now, it's used mostly at the amateur level. Sid Luckman was the first great T formation quarterback.

HB = Halfback   FB = Fullback

E = End   T = Tackle

G = Guard   C = Center

QB = Quarterback

record was declared champion without the benefit of a title game. That was something that had to change, but those running the league just didn't see it right away. The Akron (Ohio) Pros were the league's first champion based on their 8-0-1 mark. The Green Bay Packers and New York Giants joined the league in 1921, and player/coach George Halas took control of the Chicago Staleys. A year later, and forever after, they would be known as the Bears.

In 1921, Fritz Pollard was named coach while continuing to play for the Akron Pros, and he is now remembered as the first African-American to coach a league team. Then, in 1922, the league's name was changed again, this time to the National Football League, but the problem continued to be the lack of stability. In those early years

there were some strangely named teams, such as the Duluth Kelleys, Racine Legion, and Kenosha Maroons. Until there were set teams and a championship game, there was no way that the NFL could claim to be on a par with Major League Baseball, which was thriving on, among other things, the home runs of Babe Ruth.

The Game They Played

Despite franchise instability, the game being played in the early NFL was tough and rugged, and not for the faint of heart. There were now seven men on the line of scrimmage, so teams could no longer use the brutal flying wedge formation to block. With the flying wedge, offensive linemen actually linked arms and ran upfield in a V-shaped formation, protecting the running back tucked inside the V. Because offensive linemen got down very low to try to plow their way into the defenders and open holes for the running backs, it led to many serious injuries. Passing wasn't that widespread yet, but it *was* being used more in the NFL than in the colleges. And as rough as the game was, even then pass receivers could not be hit and mauled before they put a hand on the ball.

On the other side of the ball, defensive players often used their hands and went for the head and neck of the opposition. Some defensive linemen liked to completely tape their hands so they could almost use them like clubs. The center would snap the ball with his head down, looking between his legs at the quarterback's hands and hoping he could get his head up after the snap before a defender would come crashing down on it. I told you the old game was rough. Passing was done from five yards behind the line of scrimmage, and the end often split out from the line so he would have a better chance to get free for a pass.

Most teams used a formation that today is called a "tight T." The two halfbacks and the fullback were in a horizontal line several yards behind the quarterback. Sometimes the fullback stood a step or two farther back from the halfbacks. Some coaches would spread the halfbacks occasionally, and the center would pass the ball directly to the player who would run with it.

Everyone was packed so tightly on the line of scrimmage that the runners did not have a whole lot of room. The only way a runner could rip off a good gain was to make it between an offensive tackle and defensive end. But not that many players could "cut" and change direction with the swiftness and adroitness of today's backs. Teams also ran "end around" plays in which an end turned, paused a second or two, then ran toward the backfield and took a handoff from a back who was already running in the opposite direction. Done right, the defense wouldn't know for a second which player had the ball, and so there was the potential for a good gain.

There wasn't a lot of passing, so the quarterback also had to be a good runner who could take the same kind of pounding as the other backs. Touchdowns counted for six points by this time, and field goals were good for just three. Field goals were still kicked mainly by the use of the "dropkick." The kicker would get the ball with his hands out in front of him and then drop it down so the end of the ball would hit the ground first. He would time his kick to hit the ball just as it reached the ground. Jim Thorpe was one of the great dropkickers of his time and could boot long field goals using this method.

Because both lines crouched down so low and tried to hit their opponents low, there were often huge pileups at the line of scrimmage. Often, only the defensive ends and backfield men were left standing and ready to tackle the ball carrier if he, too, wasn't caught up in the pile and stopped. The huddle, still used today to call plays, also came into regular use in the 1920s. Before that, teams only gathered together before a complex or trick play. Because it was grind-it-out football with little passing, especially when the weather was bad, games were often low-scoring and grim affairs, little more than old-fashioned trench warfare.

Franchises continued to change when the 1925 season began. There were still twenty teams in one big, unmanageable division. But late in the season the league suddenly had a superstar, a player who would create newfound interest in the NFL and in professional football. He wouldn't change the league overnight, but his arrival and subsequent debut was one of the most heralded of all time. His name was Harold "Red" Grange, and they called him "The Galloping Ghost," one of the best nicknames ever. Born in Forksville, Pennsylvania, on June 13, 1903, young Harold grew up in Wheaton, Illinois. Legend has it that he got his formidable strength with a summer job that had him lugging

Leather shoulder pads, jersey, and nose guard

Harold "Red" Grange was known as the Galloping Ghost for his long, elusive runs at the University of Illinois. When he joined the Chicago Bears in 1925, there was so much fanfare that he's said to have put the NFL on the map of major American sports.

large blocks of ice. By the time he reached the University of Illinois in 1922, he was all football player—big, fast, elusive, and tough.

As a collegian he soon secured a reputation as a halfback who could break a game open at any time. Grange scored twelve touchdowns his first season with the Fighting Illini and was named an All-American. A year later, in 1924, his reputation was forever forged in the ranks of great collegiate football players. That October, Illinois went up against a powerful Michigan team that had won twenty straight games. In the first twelve minutes of play the Galloping Ghost single-handedly destroyed the Wolverines with a performance still remembered today.

Grange took the game's opening kickoff at his own 5-yard line and electrified the crowd with a 95-yard scoring jaunt. The next three times he touched the football he also scored, making long, twisting runs of fifty-six, sixty-seven, and forty-five yards. He later added a fifth touchdown and passed for a sixth. When the game ended the Galloping Ghost had run for 402 yards and Illinois had won 39-14. That performance made Red Grange the most famous football player in the country, college or pro. The celebrated sports writer Grantland Rice described Grange by writing:

A streak of fire, a breath of flame
Eluding all who reach and clutch;
A gray ghost thrown into the game
That rival hands may never touch.

Grange returned to Illinois in 1925, but the rumors about turning pro began to swirl even before the season ended. Red Grange, it was said, either had already signed a contract or was about to sign a professional contract. Of course, had he signed he could no longer have played for Illinois. The rumors continued right up until Grange finished the season for Illinois in November. His final game against Ohio State was witnessed by more than 85,000 fans as the redhead led the Illini to a 14-9 victory.

Grange had become friendly with a theatrical promoter named C.C. Pyle, nicknamed "Cash and Carry" because of his deal-making ability. In a sense, he may have been the first sports agent, and he did as well for his client as many of today's agents. Sure enough, as soon as the season ended, Red Grange and C.C. Pyle made huge headlines by signing a contact for the star half-back to play with the Chicago Bears. It was said that Grange (and Pyle, who would split the take) would get $3,000 a game or 30 percent of the gate, whichever was larger. It was the largest professional contract signed to date. Red Grange's professional debut was slated for Thanksgiving Day at Wrigley Field against the Chicago Cardinals. When the Bears played teams like the Rock Island Rockets or Duluth Eskimos, they were lucky if 5,000 fans showed up. For Red Grange's first pro game, a record NFL crowd of 36,000 fans crowded into the North Side ballpark. Almost all of them expected the 175-pound Grange to run wild.

He didn't. The field was muddy and the weather bad. Neither team could score, with Grange's longest run from scrimmage just seven

One of the great pioneers of pro football, George "Papa Bear" Halas coached the Chicago Bears on and off from 1933 to 1967.

yards. He would end up with thirty-six yards on the day but took home $12,000 for his effort. George Halas and the Bears wanted to capitalize on Grange's popularity, and they scheduled an exhausting barnstorming tour in which the team would play eight games in twelve days, covering almost every major city in the league. After that, they decided to play nine more games in the South and West. Grange and the Bears played before huge crowds everywhere. There were 73,000 fans in attendance at the Polo Grounds in New York when the Bears played the Giants, and another 75,000 at the Los Angeles Memorial Coliseum when they met the Los Angeles Tigers.

Grange made a small fortune thanks to C.C. Pyle negotiating a percentage of the gate. In New York, for example, he took home a check for $30,000. He also endorsed sportswear and soft drinks, and someone even produced a Red Grange doll. He was a modern-day athlete before modern-day athletes were invented. There was one problem. Red Grange was not proving to be the same kind of star in the pros as he was in college.

In a game against the Columbus Tigers, the Bears managed a 14-13 victory, but a Columbus halfback named Bob Rapp completely overshadowed Grange. Rapp gained 203 yards and scored one touchdown with a 61-yard jaunt. Grange's longest run was a punt return of forty-two yards and a kickoff return of twenty-eight yards. And Rapp, in the tradition of nail-tough football, played part of the game with a broken rib. And in that big game against the Giants, when Grange took home that thirty-grand check, he made no long runs, his only highlight being an intercepted pass (he played both offense and defense, as most did then) that he took untouched into the end zone. In the next game against Washington, Grange was a marked man. Defensive players had pride and didn't want this highly publicized halfback running wild on them. Hitting him hard was part of their formula for success. He would often leave the field with a badly wrenched arm, battered nose, and bruised mouth.

Stanford All-American Ernie Nevers looked tough and was tough. He hated to come out of any game and was once called "the football player without a fault." He played in the NFL from 1926 to 1931.

Pretty soon, Red Grange was exhausted. He had played a full college season and was now playing a brace of extra professional games to showcase his talents. It was too much for any man. Soon the crowds began to diminish. Only 5,000 fans showed up in Pittsburgh to watch the Bears play a team of semipros. Chicago won, 24-0, but Grange only ran for three yards, caught a pass for four, then had to leave the game with a torn muscle in his arm. He had to sit out games against Boston and Detroit for which thousands of dollars had to be refunded to fans who only came to the games to see Grange play.

Unfortunately, the Galloping Ghost would never regain his former collegiate glory. A severe knee injury cost him part of the 1927 season and all of 1928. He didn't come back until 1929, then played seven more seasons. He was no longer an amazing breakaway runner, admitting that, "After [the injury], I was just another halfback." In fact, he would turn out to be a better defensive back in the NFL than a running back. He may not have retired as a superstar, but he is still the man who single-handedly put the NFL on the map in the mid-1920s at a time the new league sorely needed a hero of epic proportion. Red Grange was surely that man.

More New Stars Arrive

With the boost in publicity pro football received from the arrival of Red Grange, the league could only continue to grow. Grange's failure to fully live up to his advance notices didn't hurt as much as some felt it would. The league had twenty-two teams in 1926, including the Duluth Eskimos, a team that had signed All-American fullback Ernie Nevers of Stanford. Nevers didn't get the kind of publicity Grange did, but he was an incredibly rugged performer. The Duluth Eskimos had only fifteen players on their team, and they would play a total of twenty-nine exhibition and league games in 1926, with twenty-eight of them being on the road. The team was nicknamed the Iron Men of the North, and no one was more durable than Nevers. He only missed a total of twenty-nine minutes in twenty-nine games. What a tribute to his toughness and grit. He was a guy who never wanted to come out of the lineup.

Nevers would forever cement his greatness on November 28, 1929. The league had contracted by then, and the big fullback was with the Chicago Cardinals. Known as "The Blond Bull," Nevers often ran behind 265-pound guard Walt Kiesling, a human battering ram who cleared the way for his fullback. On this day against the crosstown Chicago Bears, Nevers ran for six touchdowns and kicked four extra points. His total of forty points scored in a game stands as a record to this day. Nevers, however, wasn't the only new star to come into the NFL in the latter 1920s and early 1930s.

The Packers, who were beginning to make their presence felt, had a fleet halfback named John McNally. But his all-out style of play earned him a nickname that was often used more than his real surname. He was generally known as Johnny "Blood," another great football nickname. Johnny Blood also had the luxury of running behind a stellar blocker, the 6'5", 255-pound Cal Hubbard. The team also had a guy known as the game's first great blitzing linebacker, August "Mike" Michalske. The Packers would win their first championship in 1929 when the 6'0", 200-pound Blood had a fantastic game against the New York Giants. He recovered a fumble leading to the Pack's first TD, then caught a pass from Red Dunn and ran fifty-five yards for another score. The Packers won, 20-7, despite the presence of the Giants' fine quarterback, Benny Friedman, and finished the season at 12-0-1.

A year later Green Bay added quarterback Arnie Herber, perhaps the league's first real strong-armed quarterback who could throw deep, and won yet another title. That same year the Bears introduced a huge fullback/tackle named Bronko (his real name) Nagurski. This guy was born with the perfect football nickname, and it wasn't even a

John "Blood" McNally

nickname. He was the kind of stuff from which legends are made. The Bronk was 6'2", 228 pounds and had a 19-inch neck. He was as close to a human battering ram as a player could be, and it was said he could have played any position on the football field. That thought was echoed by the sportswriter Grantland Rice, who described Nagurski this way: "He was a star end, a star tackle, and a crushing fullback who could pass." Rice also wrote, "Eleven Nagurskis would be a mop-up. It would be something close to murder and massacre."

In other words, Bronko Nagurski was a complete football player. He was a great defensive player and tackler, a vicious blocker on offense, and a punishing runner who was very difficult to tackle. When he ran with the football he kept his head down and his upper body almost horizontal to the field. His knees would pump high, almost reaching his chest, and it was tough for a tackler to grab him and throw him to the ground. When a rule change was made in 1933 permitting passes from anywhere behind the line of scrimmage instead of five yards or more, Nagurski took full advantage of it. He would get the ball and charge at the line. Defenders would mass to meet him, when suddenly he would stop, jump in the air, and throw a short pass to a receiver just beyond the line.

The Bronk played for the Bears from 1930 to 1937; then he retired to become a professional wrestler. Six years later, in 1943, he came back and led the Bears to one more title before retiring once again. Though the numbers then were far short of those amassed today, Nagurski ran for 4,031 yards in his career and made defenders pay for every last one.

There were other outstanding players coming in as well during this period. Besides having more talent on the field, the league was changing in other ways. In 1927, it was decided that a 22-team league (the 1926 total) was not good for business. Financially weak teams

ROCKNE CHALLENGES THE NFL

Perhaps the strangest game of the 1930 season wasn't even on the schedule. It began when Knute Rockne, the highly successful coach at Notre Dame, began saying that a number of his great Irish teams were better than the pros. He felt professional players were not as motivated as collegians and wanted to prove it. Finally, a game was planned for New York's Polo Grounds on December 14, 1930. The proceeds from the gate would go to the New York Unemployment Fund to help those out of work because of the Great Depression. One team would consist of former Notre Dame stars who played under Rockne. The other would be the NFL New York Giants.

Rockne felt the Giants were big and slow, and his team had some outstanding former players, including the legendary backfield known as the Four Horsemen, as well as a younger group led by Frank Carideo, who Rockne called the greatest quarterback alive. But the star of the game was Giants quarterback Benny Friedman. He passed, ran, and led the Giants to an easy 22-0 victory. Many felt Benny could have run the score up even more, but he finally took himself out of the game and let the subs finish. The contest not only silenced the usually talkative Rockne but showed fans everywhere that the pros playing in the National Football League were, without a doubt, the best players in the world.

didn't do the league any good, and they diluted the talent pool. There was a slimmer look in 1927, as the NFL contracted to just twelve teams, and many of the defunct teams had been in small Midwestern cities. Now the league began settling into the larger cities in the East. The New York Giants won the championship by shutting out ten of their thirteen opponents with a great defensive effort as they completed the season with an 11-1-1 record.

The one thing the NFL still lacked was a championship game. Despite the smaller league, the teams were still lumped into one division and the team with the best record declared champion. There was nothing to compare with baseball's World Series, and it's almost amazing that someone didn't see the need for a title game of some sort. Yet the league continued to grow and refine the product. A fourth official was added in 1929, and the extra pair of eyes allowed the game to be better controlled with fewer infractions of the rules. The Providence team hosted the first night game that same year when they played the Cardinals under the lights on November 3rd. The Packers won the title shortly after the stock market crash in October and shortly before the country began sliding into the Great Depression of the 1930s.

The 1930 season was the one in which Bronko Nagurski made his debut. The Bears were also the first team to refine the T formation by splitting their ends out wide and having a halfback go in motion before the ball was snapped. But it was the Packers that won a second straight title, with rookie quarterback Arnie Herber in the lineup.

Hall of Fame fullback Bronko Nagurski ran low and hard and was very tough to tackle. Believe it or not, his real first name was Bronko. Perfect for a football player.

The Packers won a third straight title in 1931 as the league dropped to ten teams. There were only eight franchises still operating at the start of the 1932 season as the economic slowdown in the country made it tough on everyone. Then something occurred that not only impacted the future of the league but also led to one of the strangest games in NFL history. When the regular season ended, the Chicago Bears had a 6-1-6 record and the Portsmouth (Ohio) Spartans finished at 6-1-4. Tie games didn't count in the standings, so the teams were deadlocked. It was then decided the two teams should play an additional game to determine the champion. It would be, in effect, a championship game, and it was scheduled for Wrigley Field in Chicago on December 18th.

There was one problem. The weather in Chicago was bitter cold and windy, and the city was buried under a mountain of snow. The conditions were so harsh that it was decided that the game just couldn't be played outdoors. This was something, especially in an era of bad-weather football. The league decided to move the game indoors, and the only option was Chicago Stadium, which was then used mainly for hockey. Fortunately, there was already a dirt surface because the circus had just left down.

So the game was played on a field just eighty yards long, with the sidelines right up against the walls. Not surprisingly, there had to be a couple of special rules. The goalposts were moved to the goal line. On the regulation field they were still at the back of the end zone. And after a play ended near the wall, the ball was brought ten yards toward the center of the field to lessen the chance of injury. Special hash marks were drawn on both sides of the field for this purpose. The game was played before 11,198 fans, maybe more than would have braved the elements if the game were kept outdoors. Because of the small field, the offenses had trouble moving the ball. The Bears scored the only touchdown when Bronko Nagurski threw a short pass into the waiting arms of Red Grange in the end zone. A last-minute safety gave the Bears a 9-0 victory and the championship. In a strange sense, this

Because of extraordinary cold weather in Chicago, the Bears and Portsmouth Spartans had to play their 1932 playoff game for the league title indoors. The two teams clashed at Chicago Stadium, an early version of arena football, and the game also resulted in several rule changes.

game was a foreshadowing of arena football, the indoor game that wouldn't begin for more than half a century, but has since become very popular.

But this unusual game had a positive effect on the NFL. For one thing, it helped convince league bigwigs that a championship game was needed. A year later, the league was split into two divisions with the winners meeting for the NFL title. The goalposts were kept on the goal line, and the hash marks were also made a permanent part of the game so no play could begin right next to the sideline. In 1933, another

DID HIS TEAMMATES RESENT HIM?

Some feel that one reason for Red Grange's failure to duplicate his college heroics was a lack of blocking by his new teammates on the Bears. Grange was earning at least $3,000 a game, sometimes much more with his percentage of the gate. Many of his teammates, especially the guys doing the grunt work on the line, were getting just a few hundred bucks per contest. It wouldn't be surprising if some of them simply didn't go the extra mile for the hotshot runner. Because there was no championship game at that time, players could not earn extra money in the postseason. The money they earned for a game was all they would receive. And even if someone threw a good block to spring a running back then, it was usually the runner who got the credit in the papers and with the fans. So Grange simply may not have had the great support from his pro linemen that he had at Illinois when he truly was the Galloping Ghost.

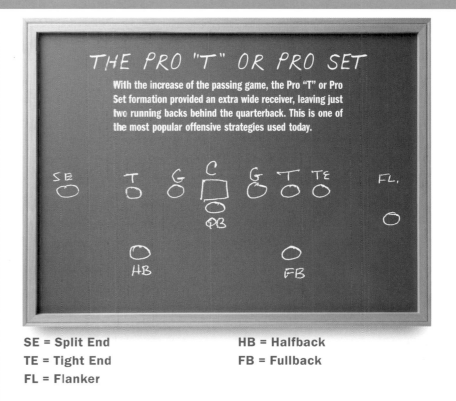

SE = Split End
TE = Tight End
FL = Flanker
HB = Halfback
FB = Fullback

rule change allowed the forward pass to be thrown anywhere behind the line of scrimmage. The passer did not have to be five yards back, as Portsmouth had argued when Nagurski threw the TD pass to Grange. So in a strange way, this game that was driven inside by the weather had a huge effect on the sport.

In 1933 the weather was better, and the Western Division champion Bears defeated the Eastern Division champion New York Giants in the first-ever NFL championship game, 23-21, at Wrigley Field. It was about time people wised up. Thanks to the addition of a championship game, a new era in professional football was about to begin.

Green Bay's Don Hutson was a pass receiver ahead of his time. He was fast, elusive, and sure-handed, a threat to score every time he caught the football. Here he grabs one on the run in a 1943 game against the Detroit Lions.

CHAPTER 3

The Road to the Modern Game

In 1934, the NFL's second championship game again was afflicted with bad weather. The result was a strange title contest decided ultimately by the footwear worn by one of the teams. The Bears, with Bronko Nagurski and a rookie runner named Beattie Feathers, had rolled through the regular season with a perfect 13-0 record. Feathers, in fact, became the first NFL runner to gain more than 1,000 yards for a season, finishing with 1,004 on just 101 carries, an average of almost ten yards a pop. Not surprisingly, the Bears were heavy favorites over the 8-5 New York Giants, winners in the East. This time the game was scheduled for the Polo Grounds and, as had happened in Chicago two years earlier, the icy weather took a hand.

The field on December 8th was frozen rock hard, so hard that the metal cleats on the players' football shoes were useless. Instead of gripping the turf, they were causing the players on both teams to slip and slide. The heavily favored Bears fared only slightly better in the first half and left the field with a 10-3 lead at intermission.

Before the game, the Giants' captain, Ray Flaherty, had suggested to Coach Steve Owen that the players wear basketball shoes—sneakers. He said his college team had once done it under similar conditions, and the sneakers gave them better traction than their cleat-wearing rivals. Coach Owen decided to try it and sent clubhouse assistant Abe Cohen to race over to nearby Manhattan College and get a batch of sneakers. Cohen returned just before the start of the second half and the New York players sorted through the pile looking for their sizes. Then they returned to the field.

The third quarter was a period of adjustment as the Giants began realizing that, yes, they could move better than the Bears. It was a 13-3 game when the final quarter began. But suddenly, the New Yorkers seemed to be floating while the Bears continued to slip and slide. First

Ed Danowski hit Ike Franklin on a 28-yard scoring pass. Then Ken Strong scored on touchdown runs of forty-two and eleven yards, and Danowski finished it off by running nine yards for the final score. Add the extra points and the Giants had scored twenty-seven unanswered fourth-quarter points to win the game and the title, 30-13.

It was the change of shoes that made the difference, and forever after this title contest has been known simply as "The Sneakers Game."

In the ensuing years, the shape of the game began to change even more because of both new rules and more complete players coming into the league. In 1935, the hash marks were moved another five yards closer to the center of the field, positioning them fifteen yards from the sidelines and keeping play closer to the middle of the field. It was also announced that beginning in 1936, NFL teams would hold an annual draft of college players, the team with the poorest record picking first. It was a way to give even the bad teams a chance to get good players.

Also that year the Packers signed a tall, 195-pound pass receiver out of the University of Alabama. Don Hutson would become known as "The Alabama Antelope" and is considered the NFL's first great pass receiver, a guy so good he could probably even play the position in today's fast-paced game. Hutson could run the 100-yard dash in 9.8 seconds, had a first-rate pair of hands, and simply couldn't be caught once he had the ball in the open field. He would catch thirty-four passes for 536 yards as a rookie as his quarterback, Arnie Herber, became the first passer to top the 1,000-yard mark. Herber completed 77 of 173 passes for 1,239 yards, and the two stars helped the Packers win the championship.

Two years later another player arrived on the scene who would also change the face of the game. He was a tailback from Texas Christian

University named Sammy Baugh, and he joined the Washington Redskins the same year the team moved to the nation's capital from Cleveland. He would be an unlikely quarterback in the NFL, as some felt he had minimal skills for the position. But Samuel Adrian Baugh was a Texan all the way, having been born in the Lone Star State town of Temple on March 17, 1914. He was a three-year star at TCU and all the while worked at improving his game.

The thin Texan would practice passing for hours on end. He suspended an old tire with a rope from a tree branch in his backyard and then tried to throw the football through the swinging tire from every angle and distance. As a pro, he never feared throwing the football. In fact, he loved it, and before long he acquired the nickname "Slingin' Sammy" Baugh. When he first joined the Redskins he operated from the tailback position, taking a direct snap from center. Like most tailbacks, Baugh could run. The difference was that the defense never knew when he was going to stop suddenly and put the football in the air.

Washington Redskins quarterback "Slingin' Sammy" Baugh was considered the first of the modern passing quarterbacks. He was also a fan favorite and loved signing autographs for his many faithful followers.

Baugh could throw on the run or could set and fling the ball downfield to a receiver. Most passers back then still threw sidearm, balancing the ball on their hands and then slinging it with a sweeping motion. Though Baugh was called "Slingin' Sammy," he didn't sling the football. Rather he threw it much like modern quarterbacks do, baseball style, bending his elbow and cocking his wrist. His passes were crisp and accurate, and it wasn't unusual for him to throw on five or six straight plays while the defense kept waiting for a run.

It was Sammy Baugh who really showed the pro football world that games could sometimes be won through prolific passing. He also brought more fans through the turnstiles because they wanted to see the football in the air, just as in the 1920s they wanted to see Babe Ruth hit home runs. Baugh threw for 1,127 yards his rookie year and

THE LOOK OF THE FUTURE

The 1937 championship game between the Redskins and Bears may well have provided the NFL with a look into the future, though no one knew it at the time. In title games played in December back then, the weather was almost always a factor. On this December 12th, the game at Wrigley Field was no exception. It was again a bitter cold and windy day, the kind of afternoon usually ready-made for grind-it-out football and low-scoring games. Only no one was really prepared for the passing wizardry of "Slingin' Sammy" Baugh.

Time after time Baugh went to the air, throwing medium and deep passes into the teeth of the wind...and completing them. The Bears simply couldn't do enough defensively to stop him. When the game ended, not only did the Redskins have a 28-21 victory, but Sammy Baugh had the kind of stats that would only appear with regularity years later. He completed seventeen of thirty-four passes for 352 yards and three touchdowns. His three scoring aerials went for fifty-five, seventy-eight, and thirty-five yards. Back then, these numbers must have seemed impossible, but Baugh had made a lot of people believers on a cold and windy day in Chicago.

led the Redskins to the championship with a 28-21 victory over the Bears in the title game. He was the real deal and would continue to lead the Redskins for the next sixteen years.

A rule change and a bonus game were the highlights of 1938. For the first time there was a 15-yard penalty for roughing the passer. That kept defenders from blasting the quarterback after he released the ball. With guys like Herber and Baugh throwing the football, the NFL brass didn't want the newfound passing game destroyed by defenders bent on putting the quarterback out of the game. It was also decided to play a game after the season between the league champion and a team of all-stars from the other teams that showcased the growing league. It would be called the Pro Bowl, and in the first one, played in January of 1939, the champion New York Giants topped the Pro All-Stars, 13-10.

The Bears got revenge on the Redskins in 1940 when they won the championship by the largest margin in NFL history, 73-0. Just three weeks earlier, in the regular season, the 'Skins had beaten Chicago, 7-3. But in the title game, everything changed. On just the second play from scrimmage, Bears fullback Bill Osmanski broke loose on a 77-yard touchdown run and the floodgates opened. It was 28-0 by the half, and Chicago continued the onslaught until the final gun. Chicago also stopped Sammy Baugh and his passing game. Baugh had a potential TD pass dropped early in the first quarter, and someone asked him if the game would have been different had it been caught.

"Yeah," Slingin' Sam answered. "It would have been 73-7."

The T Formation

The Bears had a very good quarterback of their own, Sid Luckman, who was successful because he and his team had refined the T formation. Luckman had been a triple-threat star at Erasmus Hall High School in Brooklyn and then at Columbia University. He had played halfback at both schools, and the Bears' George Halas had to convince him to play quarterback. In order to do it, Luckman had to practice taking the ball from right behind the center, then turning and giving it to his running backs. He also had to learn to drop back for a pass and pitch the ball out to a running back ten yards from him.

But he learned fast. He had been drafted in 1938, and by 1940 he had mastered his new position.

The T formation often made use of a man in motion, which served to stretch out the defense. Many teams then still used seven and eight down linemen, and they couldn't immediately deal with the man in motion. Halas supposedly discovered this by accident at practice when one of his backs

Fullback Bill Osmanski of the Chicago Bears runs upfield in a 73-0 victory over the Washington Redskins.

went in motion before the snap and the defense looked totally confused. Motion is legal when the man moves sideways or slightly backward. He cannot go in a forward direction until the ball is snapped. At any rate, to cover the man in motion a linebacker or defensive back would have to leave his position, which weakened the interior defense of a team not used to seeing this kind of formation.

If the defense simply ignored the man in motion, he would be open for a quick pass and possibly a long gain. Defenses would eventually begin playing four- and five-man lines so that more defenders would be in upright positions and ready to cope with sudden shifts and players in motion.

When the quarterback took the snap right behind the center, he was in a better position to control the play. More teams soon followed suit and began using the T formation instead of the old single-wing, in which the quarterback would take a direct snap while standing five or so yards behind the center. But to be successful with the T, a team needed a good quarterback, one who handled all aspects of the position smoothly, and Sid Luckman was the best of the emerging breed in the early 1940s. But others would surely follow.

The War Years

The 1941 season would be the last before the nation went to war. After the Japanese attack on Pearl Harbor on December 7, 1941, World War II would deplete the ranks of the NFL—as it did with Major League Baseball, as well—for the next four seasons. The Bears had a juggernaut that year, a team full of future Hall of Famers. There was Luckman at quarterback, leading an offense that would score a record 396 points in eleven games.

Because both teams finished tied at 10-1 in the regular season, the Bears had to beat the Packers in the first divisional playoff in league history, 33-14; then they whipped the Giants for the championship, 37-9. The title game came two weeks to the day after the attack on Pearl Harbor, and the country was at war.

Shortly after the 1942 season began, Bears coach George Halas left the team and became a lieutenant commander in the Navy. Many players had

George Halas & quarterback Sid Luckman

already gone, and others followed. By war's end, some 638 NFL players had served in the military, with twenty-one of them losing their lives while fighting for their country. Though the league was depleted, there were still some fine performances by the players who stayed behind between 1942-1945.

• Green Bay's Don Hutson became the first 1,000-yard receiver in 1942 when he caught seventy-four passes for 1,211 yards.

• In 1942, Cecil Isbell of the Packers became the NFL's first 2,000-yard passer, throwing for 2,021 yards on 146 completions, including a record twenty-four TD passes.

• The NFL made the wearing of helmets mandatory at the beginning of the 1943 season.

• Redskins quarterback Sammy Baugh, who played both ways like everyone else, was the top defensive back in the league in 1943 with eleven interceptions. He also led the league in passing and punting.

• Because of the dilution of talent, several teams merged to keep the league going. In 1943 Pittsburgh and Philadephia merged for one year, and a year later it was the Cardinals and the Steelers that merged.

• Chicago's Sid Luckman had the league's first 400-yard passing day on November 14, 1943, when he hit on twenty-one of thirty-two passes for 433 yards and a record seven touchdowns in a game against the New York Giants.

• In 1945, the hash marks were moved from fifteen to twenty yards in from the sidelines, again moving play closer to the center of the field and helping the offense.

• Steve Van Buren of the Philadelphia Eagles emerged as an outstanding running back, leading the league in rushing, kickoff returns, and scoring in 1945.

Heading Toward Mid-Century

In 1946, the NFL returned to normalcy with most of the players coming back from the war. The country would enter a prosperous postwar period, and the league looked to grow. Halfback Kenny Washington and end Woody Strode signed with the Los Angeles Rams and became the first African-Americans to play in the NFL in the modern era. And once again, a competing league started up.

The eight-team All-America Football Conference (AAFC) announced it would start play in 1946, and they, too, signed African-American players when fullback Marion Motley and guard Bill Willis joined the

OTHER LEAGUES

With the NFL looking more and more as if it was on the road to success in the late 1930s and early 1940s, it's not surprising that groups of people would try to start a rival league. In 1936, a league called the American Football League was formed, with the Boston Shamrocks winning its first championship. But the six-team organization only made it through one more season before disbanding. Then in 1940, another six-team American Football League was born. The Columbus Bullies won the title, but like its predecessor, this newest AFL lasted only one more year and was gone after the 1941 campaign. There had even been another AFL formed way back in 1926 that also lasted just two years. So rival leagues had a two-years-and-out pattern, but these wouldn't be the last efforts to rival the NFL, and eventually, beginning in 1960, one would finally be successful.

new Cleveland Browns. Because there was more prosperity in the country after the war and more fans, the AAFC would persevere and become a bona fide rival to the NFL.

The Giants beat the Bears, 24-14, to win the first postwar championship, but the NFL had a major concern with the new AAFC. The new league put teams in four NFL markets—Los Angeles, Chicago, New York, and Cleveland. In fact, they had Cleveland all to themselves because the Cleveland Rams had moved to Los Angeles. Both leagues began vying for top players, and the AAFC was also taking some players from the NFL, such as quarterback Clarence "Ace" Parker. But perhaps the biggest story, and the one that made the NFL really take notice, was the juggernaut team being put together by Coach Paul Brown in Cleveland.

Otto Graham had been a utility back at Northwestern University, usually running and blocking but throwing an occasional pass as

Cleveland Browns fullback Marion Motley helped his team dominate the All-America Football Conference and then later the NFL.

STEVE VAN BUREN PROVES HIS METTLE

The 1949 title game had the 11-1 Philadelphia Eagles going up against the 8-2-2 Los Angeles Rams. The December game was scheduled for the Los Angeles Coliseum, where the weather was usually beautiful, sunny, and balmy. That made the NFL brass happy because it was slated to be the first NFL title game to be televised from coast to coast. They also expected a live gate of 60,000 or more fans. The Rams had a quick-strike team led by the quarterback tandem of Bob Waterfield and Norm Van Brocklin. The Eagles were led by quarterback Tommy Thompson, end Pete Pihos, and an exceptional halfback named Steve Van Buren.

Many call Van Buren the first modern NFL running back. At 6'0", 208 pounds, Van Buren had that special combination of speed, power, and cutting ability. During the regular season he had set a rushing mark with 1,146 yards, the result of his intense training methods. In the summers, Van Buren would run the beaches near Cape May, New Jersey, twice a day, plowing through the soft sand in his high-top football shoes and sometimes even strapping weights to his ankles. He was always ready for anything.

Many call Philadelphia Eagles halfback Steve Van Buren the first of pro football's modern runners. He was big, fast, and strong, gaining 196 yards in the mud and rain to lead the Eagles to a victory in the 1949 NFL title game.

What no one was ready for was the weather. On the day of the game Los Angeles was inundated by torrential rains. Rams officials wanted the game postponed, but the NFL was committed to TV and radio deals. So it was played on a field that was soft, wet, and muddy—a real quagmire. Only some 35,000 fans braved the weather, and what they ended up seeing was the Steve Van Buren show.

While the Rams' passing attack fizzled in the rain, and power runners Tank Younger and Dick Hoerner had trouble getting their footing, Van Buren simply rumbled over everyone. All those days running on the sand had paid off. He ripped off one good gain after another, controlling the ball and the game. Philly won the title 14-0 as Steve Van Buren gained an amazing 196 yards on thirty-one carries, records for a championship game that would last for twenty-five years.

Steve Van Buren's career was ultimately shortened by a knee injury, but he was the best running back of the 1940s and proved it once and for all on a rainy, muddy field in Los Angeles, where he stood head and shoulders above all the rest.

well. Paul Brown saw some real innate ability in Graham. He was tall, strong, and fast, and had amazing peripheral vision. Brown envisioned him as a quarterback of unlimited potential and was right. He surrounded Graham with a couple of fast and talented receivers—Dante Lavelli and Mac Speedie—and then put together a backfield that included the powerful, tough, and determined Marion Motley at fullback. Add a solid offensive line and a great defense, and the Browns quickly become the class of the new league.

This was a dominant football team that would win four consecutive AAFC championships. In fact, they were so much better than the other teams in the league that it almost killed fan interest. The team would win an amazing fifty-two games and lose just four, along with a pair of ties, in four seasons. No football team, before or since, has been that dominant.

Meanwhile, the NFL carried on, and the rule changes and innovations continued. A fifth official, a back judge, was added in 1947, and a flexible artificial tee was allowed to be used on kickoffs in 1948. That same year halfback Fred Gehrke of the Los Angeles

Otto Graham was a resourceful quarterback and accurate passer who played his best in the biggest games. He led the Cleveland Browns to championships in both the AAFC and NFL, and himself to the Hall of Fame.

Rams painted horns on all his team's helmets, the first emblem or team logo on a helmet in NFL annals. Free substitution was adopted for one year in 1949, and a year later it became permanent, opening the doors to the coming era of separate offensive and defensive units and eventual specialization in the pro game.

On the field, the weather played a factor in two title games. In 1948, the Philadelphia Eagles defeated the Chicago Cardinals 7-0 for the title in a game played during a blizzard. A year later, it was the Eagles and Rams in Los Angeles playing their title game in a heavy rainstorm on a soft, muddy field. Also in 1949, the NFL had two 1,000-yard rushers for the first time, as both Steve Van Buren of Philadelphia and Tony Canadeo of Green Bay topped the mark.

The big news, however, came on December 9th, two days before the championship game. NFL Commissioner Bert Bell announced a merger agreement with the AAFC in which three of the rival conference teams—the Cleveland Browns, San Francisco 49ers, and Baltimore Colts—would join the NFL in 1950. The AAFC was the first competing league to force the older league's hand, but it probably could not have survived on its own, and these three teams would only strengthen the NFL.

The 1930s and 1940s were a period of real growth for the National Football League, a time when the game moved into the modern era and became an established big-time professional sport. There were great impact players like Sammy Baugh and Steve Van Buren, the advent of the championship game, important rule changes, and a stabilized league. The upcoming merger with the All-America Football Conference would add new teams for 1950, including one that would further change the game. The NFL now stretched from coast to coast, talented players would continue to emerge, more television coverage was coming soon, and in the next decade the game would become bigger than ever before.

Dante Lavelli was a fine pass receiver for the Cleveland Browns during their early dynasty years in the AAFC and then the NFL.

CHAPTER 4

Though this chapter encompasses a relatively short time frame, it is nonetheless a very important one. This period began and ended with two of the most dramatic and important championship titles in league history, and in between introduced a whole new group of great, record-setting players. There was a thirteen-team league at the beginning of the 1950 season, including the three teams from the now defunct All-America Football Conference (AAFC). With one exception, these were all bona fide NFL franchises that are still in existence today, though a couple have moved to other cities.

The American Conference included the New York Giants, Philadelphia Eagles, Pittsburgh Steelers, Chicago Cardinals, Washington Redskins, and the AAFC Cleveland Browns. The National Conference consisted of the Los Angeles Rams, Chicago Bears, New York Yankees, Detroit Lions, Green Bay Packers, and the AAFC San Francisco 49ers and Baltimore Colts. San Francisco and Baltimore would have difficulty adjusting to NFL play and finish a combined 4-20 on the season. But the Cleveland Browns were a totally different story.

The Browns brought with them the reputation of being a dominant team. Their stellar record in the AAFC was well documented, and the team had the swagger of a champion. NFL stalwarts had always felt their league was superior and hoped the Browns would get a quick comeuppance. The perfect team to do it was waiting for them in the season opener—the NFL champion Philadelphia Eagles. The game was set for September 16th, in Philly. It was a Saturday night and the eyes of all football fans would be watching. Most felt the NFL Eagles would show these upstart Browns how the game was really played.

Cleveland still had the core group that allowed them to dominate the AAFC, led by Otto Graham at quarterback. Marion Motley was a bruising fullback, while Dante Lavelli and Mac Speedie were as good as anyone at ends. Coach Paul Brown had developed a sophisticated passing attack that featured the hook, or come-back pattern, as well as a wide variety of sideline throws. The Browns also used men in motion, ran a power sweep, and controlled the line with the bull-like rushes of Motley. Coach Brown was always prepared and had his assistants scouting top NFL teams even before the merger.

Philadelphia was at an immediate disadvantage. Steve Van Buren, their great running back, would miss the game due to injury. Still, the team was supremely confident because they simply didn't think an AAFC team could be that good. Paul Brown, however, admitted he had been waiting for this moment for a long time.

"It was the highest emotional game I ever coached," he said. "We had four years of constant ridicule to get us ready. "

The Eagles scored first on a 13-yard field goal by Cliff Patton midway through the first quarter, but the Browns were just warming up. Before the period ended Graham noticed an Eagles defensive back playing too close to receiver Dub Jones. He called Jones' number, hit him with a pass as soon as he got behind his defender, and it turned into a 59-yard touchdown play. The kick made it 7-3. Then in the second quarter the Browns' QB found Dante Lavelli open for a 26-yard score and a 14-3 halftime lead.

Early in the third period Cleveland did it again as Paul Brown outfoxed Coach Greasy Neale and the Eagles. He moved halfback Rex Bumgardner into Motley's fullback spot, put him in motion, and Graham hit him three straight times for thirty yards before Philly could adjust. After a 32-yard completion to Lavelli, the cagey Graham hit Mac Speedie from twelve yards out for yet another score. It was now 21-3, and NFL stalwarts were shaking their heads in disbelief.

The final was 35-10, leaving no doubt that the Cleveland Browns could compete with, and probably beat, anyone.

The Browns went on to compile a 10-2 record in their first NFL season, being nearly as dominant as they were in the AAFC. Their success only served to spark new interest in the league. So did television. The Rams became the first team to have all their games—both home and away—televised, and soon the Redskins were following suit. It would start a trend as more teams began televising some or all of their games. The sport played well on the small screen and more fans became aware of professional gridiron action every week.

Los Angeles Rams quarterback Bob Waterfield (7) gets set to make a tackle in a 1950 game against Baltimore. Like other QBs of that era, Waterfield played defense as well as offense.

When the season ended there was added excitement. The Browns and Giants both finished at 10-2 in the American Conference, while the Rams and Bears were deadlocked at 9-3 in the National. That meant an extra set of playoff games in which the Browns and Rams prevailed. Now the tension built again. The Rams had lost the mud game to the Eagles the year before and wanted the title badly. As for the Browns, they were trying to do what was first thought impossible—win a championship their first year in the league.

This was a game that would feature eight future Hall of Famers. There was quarterback Graham, fullback Motley, tackle/placekicker Lou Groza, and end Dante Lavelli of the Browns. The Rams had their quarterback tandem of Waterfield and Van Brocklin, as well as pass receivers Tom Fears and Elroy "Crazylegs" Hirsch. All were terrific players.

Los Angeles had scored 486 points in twelve games, their two quarterbacks throwing for 3,709 yards, but Cleveland also had a fine offense, led by the talented and wily Graham. The Browns' forte, however, was defense. The defensive unit had yielded just 144 points in the regular season. But could they stop the dazzling attack of the Rams?

The game was played on December 24, 1950, on the frozen turf of Cleveland Stadium. On the first play from scrimmage quarterback Waterfield hit halfback Glenn Davis down the left sideline near midfield. The speedy Davis turned on the burners and rambled all the way to the end zone to complete an 82-yard touchdown play. The kick made it 7-0. Thanks to that one play, many thought the Rams were about to unmask the Browns as pretenders.

But Cleveland didn't rattle. Led by Graham, the Browns drove downfield and scored on a 31-yard pass from Graham to Dub Jones. Groza's kick tied it at 7-7. Then, before the quarter ended, L.A. scored again, this time on a Dick Hoerner run. It looked as if it was going to be a big offensive day, which would favor the Rams. Then Cleveland got the only score of the second quarter on a 26-yard TD pass to Lavelli. Groza missed the kick, and at halftime the Rams had a 14-13 lead.

In the third quarter the Rams increased their lead to 28-20, paving the way for a wild finish. Five minutes into the final quarter, Browns defensive back Warren Lahr intercepted a Waterfield pass, and Cleveland began driving immediately with Otto Graham taking charge. On a fourth-and-four play, he passed seven yards for the first down. Then on a subsequent fourth-and-three, he ran it himself for yet another first down. Finally, on the eighth play of the drive Graham calmly hit Rex Bumgardner from nineteen yards out for the score. The kick made it a 28-27 game.

Then the Browns got the ball back with just 1:50 left, still sixty-eight yards from the Rams' goal line. Graham ran first for fourteen yards, and then threw to Bumgardner for fifteen yards and to Jones for sixteen more. With one minute left, the Browns were at the L.A. 23-yard line. Graham dropped back once again and hit Bumgardner for another twelve yards, bringing the ball to the 11-yard line. Timeout. After one more play to move the ball closer to the center of the field, Groza then came in and booted a 16-yard field goal to give the Browns a 30-28 lead with twenty-eight seconds left. His kick turned out to be the game winner.

The game was an exciting end to a season and a strong start to a new decade. The Browns had proved they were winners in any league, and the Rams also showed the football world the skill levels to which the world's greatest players had risen. The NFL couldn't have been happier.

A Decade Evolves

The pro game was now evolving quickly. Television was helping to create new fans, and all the small-town teams were gone. Most games were being played in large stadiums with capacities for more than 50,000 fans. New rivalries were beginning to build, and while the Cleveland Browns had emerged as a super team, there were a number of other clubs that would challenge them for football supremacy.

The game continued to evolve. In 1951, a rule was passed making interior offensive linemen—the tackles, guards, and center—ineligible to receive a forward pass, another step toward specialization. A year later, the Pittsburgh Steelers became the last NFL team to stop using the old single-wing formation, in which the quarterback stood five or six yards behind the center and took a direct snap. Now, all teams use the T formation with the quarterback right under the center.

One of the best of the new T formation quarterbacks was Bobby Layne, who joined the Detroit Lions out of the University of Texas in 1950. Supremely confident in his abilities to lead a football team, Layne once supposedly said, "I never lost a game. Sometimes, I just ran out of time." With Layne at the helm, the Detroit Lions became champions in 1952 and 1953, defeating the still-potent Browns in the title game both times.

Also in 1953, the names of the two divisions were changed from the American and National to the Eastern and Western Conferences. Records continued to be set in 1954 when fullback Joe "The Jet" Perry of the San Francisco 49ers became the first back in league history to gain more than 1,000 yards rushing in two consecutive seasons. Cleveland rebounded to reclaim the championship with a 56-10 victory over Detroit, and they won it again the next year, 1955, with a 38-14 triumph over the Rams. With that game, the Browns' quarterback Otto Graham retired after leading his team to ten championship games in ten years, first in the AAFC and then in the NFL. His next stop would be the Pro Football Hall of Fame.

Detroit Lions quarterback Bobby Layne (22) gets set to launch one downfield. Layne was one of the top signal callers of the 1950s, a player who loved to party but also hated to lose football games.

But the league wouldn't be strapped for stars. Graham's successor as the next star quarterback had already joined the Baltimore Colts, after an eighty-cent long-distance phone call plucked him off the sandlots in Pittsburgh. And two years later, a man still called the best running back in the history of the game would join the Cleveland Browns after a storied career at Syracuse University. John Unitas and Jim Brown were about to begin redefining greatness.

Moving Toward Another Terrific Title Game

In 1956, a 6'1", 195-pound, stoop-shouldered quarterback appeared on the Baltimore Colts roster. The fact that he was there at all surprised a lot of people. John Constantine Unitas had played his college ball at the University of Louisville, a school not known for producing NFL stars. He was a ninth-round pick of the Pittsburgh Steelers in 1955 and was unceremoniously cut from the team. Unitas then began playing semipro ball for the Bloomfield Rams in Pittsburgh for the grand sum of six dollars per week. But when the Colts' George Shaw was injured, the team made its famous eighty-cent phone call and invited Johnny U. to join them. He won the regular job in 1956 and a year later became the league's Most Valuable Player.

The same year Unitas won the MVP prize, the Cleveland Browns unveiled an incredible running back. Jim Brown was 6'2" and 232 pounds of sculpted muscle,

The legendary John Unitas (19), shown throwing in traffic during the Baltimore Colts 1958 title game against the New York Giants. Unitas led his team to victory in sudden-death overtime and is still called the best ever by many fans of the game.

a natural athlete who was as fast as he was strong. He could overpower linemen and linebackers, run away from speedy safeties, and change direction on a dime. He had perfect balance and a winner's temperament. Brown hated to be stopped for no gain and hated even more to lose yardage. He led the league in rushing as a rookie with 942 yards, including a single-game mark of 237 yards in thirty-one attempts against the Rams. And he was just getting started.

There were some other fine runners in the league then, players like Hugh "The King" McElhenny, Joe Perry, Frank Gifford, and Ollie Matson. But Brown had all the attributes of the others plus some more of his own. He was, in effect, in a class by himself. He would prove it in his second season of 1958 when he set a new single-season rushing mark with 1,527 yards in twelve games. Brown carried the ball 257 times and averaged an impressive 5.9 yards a carry. In addition, he scored seventeen touchdowns.

Just as the 1950 season produced two pivotal games, the 1958 season provided an incredible ending. The first was for the Eastern Conference crown, and the second was an epic championship game that may have meant more to the ultimate success of the National Football League than any single game ever before. In the regular season, the New York Giants and Cleveland Browns battled tooth and nail for the top spot all season long. Cleveland, with Jim Brown, had the better offense, while the Giants tended to rely on its defense to carry the day.

In the Western Conference, the Baltimore Colts, with John Unitas really coming into his own, were trying to fend off both the Chicago Bears and Los Angeles Rams. All five contenders had outstanding football teams, and the races in both divisions created interest and excitement. When the smoke cleared, the Giants and Browns were tied in the East with identical 9-3 records while the Colts, also at 9-3,

IS HE HURT? IS HE TIRED?

Jim Brown is still widely considered the greatest running back ever to don cleats and pads. When the handsome Brown retired from the Cleveland Browns to pursue a movie career after the 1965 season, he was the NFL's all-time leading rusher and never missed a single game to injury.

Even in his second year, Jim Brown had a trait that would continue throughout his great career. Though a marked man by opposing defenses, he would fight and claw for every yard. Sometimes it would take three, four, or even five defensive players to bring him down. When that happened, Brown would often stay on the ground for several seconds, making everyone wonder if he was hurt. Then he would get up very slowly, almost painfully. He would walk back to the huddle with the tentative gait of an old man and, until they knew his MO, the defenders sometimes felt they had him on the ropes. Then, the next time he got the ball, he came back at them faster and harder than the play before. Soon, they knew the truth. Brown was either playing possum or just following a longtime habit. Maybe it was his way to get a bit of rest. But Jim Brown was never tired, and rarely hurt. He just liked to get up slowly, take his time getting back to the huddle, and be ready for the next play. Then, BOOM!

edged both the 8-4 Bears and Rams to reach the title game. In the East, however, there would be a playoff for the crown.

To force the playoff, however, the Giants had to beat the Browns in the final regular-season game. Not many people thought they could beat Jim Brown and company twice in a row to win the Eastern crown.

The season-ending game with the Browns was held at a snow-swept Yankee Stadium on December 14, 1958. It was brutal football weather, and as the game wore on neither team could really get the offense going on the slippery turf. On the first play of the game, however, Jim Brown showed all his impressive talents by running sixty-five yards for a touchdown and a 7-0 Cleveland lead. But for the remainder of the first half Cleveland's Lou Groza and the Giants' Pat Summerall managed just a field goal apiece, and it was 10-3, Browns, at intermission.

At the half, Giants receiver Kyle Rote told his quarterback, Charley Conerly, that the Browns were vulnerable to a halfback option pass because they were coming up close to try to force a sweep. He felt he could get open, and the Giants decided to wait for just the right time. It was still 10-3 and about five minutes into the fourth quarter when Jim Brown slipped on the snowy field and fumbled. The Giants got the ball at the Cleveland 45-yard line. On the first play, quarterback Conerly flipped the ball to Frank Gifford, who began to circle the right side with three blockers ahead of him. Suddenly he pulled up and fired the ball downfield. Rote caught it in full stride and was dragged down from behind at the Browns' 6-yard line.

On third and goal, the Giants ran the same play, and Gifford hit tight end Bob Schnelker in the end zone. Touchdown! Summerall's extra point tied the game at 10-10. Because there was no sudden-death overtime in the regular season then, a tie would give the Browns the title. The Giants' last chance rested on Pat Summerall kicking a 49-yard field goal in worsening weather conditions.

The snow was falling harder, the stadium darkening, and the footing nearly impossible when Summerall and his holder, Charley Conerly, set up. Conerly caught the snap, put the ball down, and Summerall stepped into it. It started end over end toward the distant goalposts.

"As soon as I hit it, I knew it would be far enough," Summerall would say later. "But from that distance a ball often has a tendency to float, like a knuckleball. I watched it all the way, and as it passed the ten-yard line, I could see that it was inside the left upright. Then it straightened itself out and was okay."

The kick was good. The Giants had won, and the Eastern Division ended in a tie. There would have to be a playoff game for the crown, as

THE "I" FORMATION

The modern "I" formation features a running back at the tailback (TB) position. He usually carries the football while the fullback (FB) is generally used as a blocking back. This formation can be used for both passing and a power running attack.

S.E.   T G C G T TE   FL.

QB

FB

TB

SE = Split End
TE = Tight End
FL = Flanker

FB = Fullback
TB = Tailback

Summerall's clutch kick quickly became legend. A week later the Giants' defense did it again. New York won the playoff game 10-0, their defense amazingly holding Jim Brown to a mere eight yards rushing. The Giants were conference champs and would now meet the Baltimore Colts for the league championship.

A Game for the Ages

The Giants had won the NFL title two years earlier, blasting the Bears 47-7, and they hoped to do the same against the Colts. But Baltimore, under Coach Weeb Ewbank, had a powerhouse team that scored a league-best 381 points in the regular season. Besides Unitas, the team had an explosive halfback in Lenny Moore, who could both run the ball and catch it deep; an all-pro receiver in Raymond Berry, who always seemed to be open; and a pile-driving fullback named Alan "The Horse" Ameche. But the Colts also had a fine defense, one that allowed just 203 regular-season points, second only to the Giants. Their defensive stars were tackles Art Donovan and Gene "Big Daddy" Lipscomb, tough-as-nails end Gino Marchetti, and linebackers Don Shinnick and Bill Pellington. All rough customers. The game was considered a real toss-up and was played on a cold December 28th, with some 64,175 fans filling Yankee Stadium.

The Giants took the early lead on a Summerall field goal, but in the second quarter Unitas led the Colts to a pair of scores, giving Baltimore a 14-3 advantage at halftime. The Giants closed to 14-10 at the end of three quarters to make it anyone's game. Then, at the outset of the fourth quarter, Conerly hit Gifford with a 15-yard touchdown pass, and the Giants again had the lead, 17-14.

Now the defense took over. Twice the Giants' "D" rose to the occasion and stopped Baltimore drives before the team could get on the scoreboard. The Giants had a chance to run out the clock, but on a third-and-four at the 40-yard line, Marchetti and Lipscomb combined to stop a Gifford run just inches short of a first down. The Giants elected to punt. Don Chandler's boot led to a fair catch at the 14-yard line. The Colts now had just 1:56 left to get a tying field goal or winning touchdown. Against the rock-ribbed Giants defense that was a tall order to fill.

That's when young John Unitas really went to work, showing the football world a combination of coolness under pressure, ultimate skill, and the nerves of a riverboat gambler. Never one to talk much, Unitas always declined to speak to his teammates before a game. Instead he would quip, "Talk is cheap. Let's play." Now, with the

DEE-FENSE! DEE-FENSE! DEE-FENSE!

Traditionally, the eyes of most football fans were always on the offense. Nothing excited the crowds like an electrifying running back, explosive passer, or acrobatic wide receiver. Those players were always the focal points. But in 1958, things began changing, especially in New York. Giants defensive coach Tom Landry (who would soon be guiding the expansion Dallas Cowboys) had molded a strong defensive unit that featured four down linemen and three linebackers. This "4-3" defense would soon become standard around the league. In addition to yielding a league-low 183 points during the regular season, the defense had a number of high-profile players, led by middle linebacker Sam Huff. Soon, fans in New York loved to see their defense trotting onto the field, and whenever the game was close they would begin chanting: DEE-FENSE! DEE-FENSE! DEE-FENSE!

championship on the line, he played. He drove the Colts downfield, connecting on several clutch passes with Raymond Berry. With just thirty seconds left, Steve Myhra came on and kicked a clutch, 20-yard field goal to tie the game at 17-17.

Of that drive, Unitas would later say, "We were so disgusted with ourselves that when we got the ball for that last series, we struck back at the Giants in a sort of blind fury."

Seconds later the gun sounded and, for the first time in NFL history, a championship would be decided by sudden-death overtime. In other words, the first team that scored in any way, shape, or form would win the game.

The Giants won the coin toss and elected to receive the football at the start of the overtime period. This time they couldn't get a first down, falling a yard short and forced to punt. Chandler's boot pinned the Colts back at their 20-yard line, and Unitas shuffled out onto the field once again. After L.G. Dupre gained eleven yards and a first down, the Colts then faced a third-and-eight. Unitas threw a flare to fullback Ameche, who ran for a first down. When he was sacked for an 8-yard loss, the redoubtable quarterback came right back and passed to Raymond Berry for a clutch, 21-yard gain to the Giants' 42-yard line. With the Giants looking for another pass, Unitas gave the ball to Ameche, who rambled twenty-three yards up the middle to get another first down at the 19-yard line.

Seconds later, Unitas hit Berry again, this time just eight yards from the end zone. The Colts could have tried for a winning field goal, but Unitas had the momentum going his way. He stayed on the field and promptly hit tight end Jim Mutscheller on the sideline. He was pushed out of bounds at the one. Unitas then gave the ball to his big fullback once again, and Ameche bulled his way into the end zone for the winning score.

"When I slapped the ball into Ameche's belly and saw him take off, I knew nobody was going to stop him," Unitas said.

The Colts celebrated before the disappointed Giants and their fans. Unitas had completed twenty-six of forty passes for 349 yards, and Berry had grabbed twelve of them for 178 yards in a great performance. But in a sense, however, there really wasn't a loser. All of pro football had been the winners. The National Football League had just put on a nationally televised show that in the eyes of many finally put the sport on par with Major League Baseball and its World Series. Defensive players had become stars and personalities in their own right, and John Unitas was well on his way to becoming a legend.

Even today, the 1958 championship game is looked upon as special, and there are fans everywhere who still call it The Greatest Game Ever Played!

Green Bay coach Vince Lombardi was a taskmaster who knew how to build winning teams. Here he watches his Packers run onto the field before the start of the 1966 NFL title game against the Dallas Cowboys. Number 75 is the outstanding tackle Forrest Gregg.

CHAPTER 5

Lombardi, the Packers & the Super Bowl

During the 1959 season two things happened that would reshape the pro football landscape over the next decade, and they had nothing to do with the race to the championship. It really wasn't surprising that the Colts repeated as champions, defeating the Giants for the second time in a row, this time by a 31-16 score. That game firmly established John Unitas as the best quarterback in the game and the Colts as the best team in the league. But much of that was about to change.

On January 28, 1959, long before the season began, it was announced that Vince Lombardi had been named the new coach of the lowly Green Bay Packers. The once-proud franchise had fallen on hard times, finishing the 1958 season with a 1-10-1 record.

Lombardi, who was born in Brooklyn, New York, on June 11, 1913, was a lifelong football man. He was an outstanding lineman at Fordham University, then he became an assistant coach there and later at West Point. In 1954, he moved on to become an assistant with the New York Giants, and many felt he would be the team's next head coach. Then Green Bay called.

The first time he met with his new team, Lombardi supposedly looked at the ragtag bunch in front of him and then held up a ball. "Gentlemen," he said. "This is a football, and before we're through, we're gonna run it down everyone's throats." He also told them he had never been associated with a losing team and wasn't about to begin now.

Lombardi went right to work. He quickly got rid of players who didn't fit his mold, who didn't want to win badly enough, or who weren't willing to make the sacrifices he demanded. In his first season at the helm, the Packers surprised everyone by finishing with a 7-5 record.

The team played basic football, preferring to establish the run before taking to the air. The new coach was a taskmaster and a drill sergeant, a psychologist and a father figure. He would do whatever it took to win, and the players who stuck with him not only came to respect him as a coach but loved him as a man, as well.

But Lombardi wasn't the only news in 1959. That summer Lamar Hunt of Dallas and Kenneth S. "Bud" Adams of Houston both gave up on the idea of getting NFL franchises for their cities. Instead, they announced they would start a new league in 1960. It would be called the American Football League (AFL), a name used several times before by leagues that tried to compete with the NFL and failed. But Hunt and Adams were resolute, and by the fall of 1960 eight franchises were ready to begin operation. The NFL had a new rival.

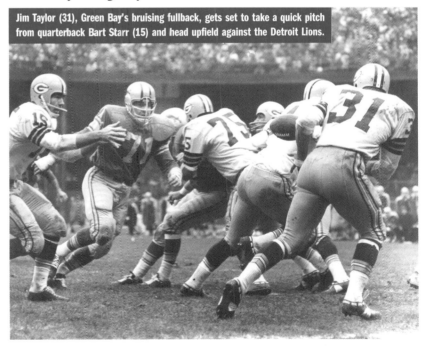

Jim Taylor (31), Green Bay's bruising fullback, gets set to take a quick pitch from quarterback Bart Starr (15) and head upfield against the Detroit Lions.

The New League Is for Real

The new AFL got a real boost in June of 1960 when it signed a five-year deal worth some $9 million to have its games televised on ABC. TV was becoming a big part of pro football by this time, and having their games broadcast could only help. Sure enough, the new league began play on September 9th, with Eastern Conference franchises in Houston, New York City, Buffalo, and Boston. The Western Conference teams were in Los Angeles, Dallas, Oakland, and Denver. The NFL had also made a couple of changes, moving the Chicago Cardinals to St. Louis and adding a new team in Dallas. The Cowboys were coached by former Giants defensive coach Tom Landry and would finish 1-11-1 in their first season.

But one way or another, pro football was getting bigger. The NFL now had thirteen teams; the AFL joined in with eight. However, the product that the AFL put on that first season was clearly not up to NFL standards. There simply weren't enough good players to go around. Another question was whether the new league could survive by playing in some small and antiquated stadiums and in front of sparse crowds. Obviously, they had to put a better brand of football on the field. The Houston Oilers would win the first AFL title, defeating the Los Angeles Chargers 24-16 before 32,183 fans. It wasn't like an NFL championship crowd, but the league had made it through its first season and would return in 1961.

Not surprisingly, the most excitement was created in the NFL, where Vince Lombardi, in just his second year as their coach, had the Packers in the title game. The Packers finished at 8-4, scoring the second-most points in the league and allowing the second fewest. It was an amazing turnaround. The Pack would be meeting the 10-2 Philadelphia Eagles, quarterbacked by Norm Van Brocklin, and with a team of veterans that came together for one amazing season. Meanwhile, the Packers' backfield of quarterback Bart Starr, halfback Paul Hornung, and fullback Jim Taylor were an improving lot, as were the rest of the Packers under Lombardi's deft and often tough hand.

The title game went down to the wire. The Eagles had a 17-13 lead with more than nine minutes left in the final period. Three times the Packers began driving. One drive was stopped when Philly middle linebacker Chuck Bednarik recovered a fumble. The next two died on downs. Then, with just 1:30 left, quarterback Starr began driving the Packers one last time, starting from his own 35-yard line. He moved his club past the 50-yard line and toward the Eagles' goal line. Finally, the ball was on the Eagles' 22-yard line with seventeen seconds left and no timeouts.

Starr called signals, took the snap, and after a look to the end zone, threw an outlet pass to fullback Taylor. With his eye on the goal line, the bull-like Taylor broke through two defenders and now had one man to beat, the veteran Bednarik, who was at the 9-yard line. The old-school Bednarik took Taylor to the ground with a brilliant tackle, then literally sat on top of the squirming Taylor until the gun sounded. The Eagles were champs.

Over the next several seasons the landscape of professional football began changing very rapidly. Lombardi's transformation of the Packers became complete when they defeated the Giants in the 1961 title game 37-0. The third-year coach had quickly put together a power-house team on both offense and defense. The Pack would win the NFL championship again in 1962, then three more from 1965 to 1967.

In the meantime, the young American Football League was having growing pains, but surviving. In January of 1961, end Willard Dewveall of the Bears played out his option and signed with the

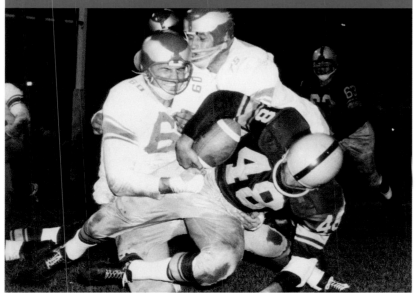
Hall of Fame linebacker Chuck Bednarik (60) makes a tackle for the Eagles in a 1958 game against the Packers. In the 1960 NFL championship game, Bednarik played both center and linebacker as the Eagles defeated Green Bay. In that game, he became the last of the two-way players, going the distance on both offense and defense.

Houston Oilers, becoming the first player to move from one league to the other. It made many teams fear that a money war for the best players would be coming very soon. Then by 1963, the Dallas Texans moved to Kansas City and became the Chiefs. The New York Titans, with serious money problems, were sold to a new group of owners headed by David "Sonny" Werblin. Weeb Ewbank, who had coached the Baltimore Colts to a sudden-death win over the Giants in 1958, became the new head coach, and the team's name was changed to the Jets. A year later they would move into the brand-new Shea Stadium, which the team would share with Major League Baseball's Mets.

By 1964, the AFL had signed a five-year, $36 million television deal with NBC to begin the following year, and more and more it began to look as if the new league was going to make it. The TV money was all-important to their survival, and now they had it. On the field, the new league still didn't have as many top-level players as in the older league, and to counter that they gave fans a wide-open, high-scoring game with more deep passing and quick-striking offenses. They also had the option of running or passing for a two-point conversion as opposed to the traditional and almost automatic point-after place-kick that had long been an NFL tradition. The league also began making a concerted effort to sign highly skilled, passing quarterbacks, even taking a couple of vets from the NFL, like Tobin Rote, who went from Detroit to San Diego and led the Chargers to a 51-10 victory over Boston to win the 1963 AFL championship.

In 1964, the Buffalo Bills signed a placekicker out of Cornell University who would also change the game of football. His name was Pete Gogolak, and he was the first of the so-called soccer-style place-kickers. Traditional, "straight-ahead" kickers like Lou "The Toe" Groza stood directly behind the football, stepped into it, and kicked it with their toes. Gogolak stood off to the side and swept his leg across his body, hitting the football with the instep instead of the toe. It was the same way a soccer ball was kicked. Gogolak would set a pro record in 1965 by booting twenty-eight field goals. Soon, it became widely acknowledged that the soccer-style kickers were more accurate and had greater range. In today's game, all placekickers boot the ball in this way.

So the AFL continued to flourish, and by 1965 the war to sign the best college players was really heating up. Because each league had separate drafts, the top college players suddenly had a choice between the NFL and AFL teams that had both picked them. Let the bidding begin. It reached a point early in 1965 when a strong-armed, charismatic quarterback came out of the University of Alabama. His contract would not only set a signing record but would signal to both leagues that something had to be done, that a truce had to be reached before they went broke.

Great Players Come and Go

In many ways, the mid-1960s also represented a changing of the guard as far as the star players in the pro game were concerned. Norm Van Brocklin, for example, who had started with the L.A. Rams in the late 1940s, retired after leading the Philadelphia Eagles to the 1960 championship. A year later, a rookie quarterback began playing for the expansionist Minnesota Vikings. His name was Fran Tarkenton and, unlike traditional quarterbacks who stood almost immobile in the "pocket" looking to pass, Tarkenton ran all over the place. They soon called him "Fran the Scram," and he became the first of the scrambling quarterbacks, showing the football world that a quarterback could move around in the backfield, throw on the run, and still be effective. He went on to have an extraordinary career.

In 1963, the great Jim Brown set a new NFL rushing mark by gaining 1,863 yards in fourteen games, the regular-season schedule having been expanded by two games in 1961. He was as close to unstoppable as any running back ever. Brown led the league again in 1964 and 1965. After the 1965 season he signed a contract to star in a motion picture. Hollywood saw the handsome, charismatic Brown as a potential action star. When the filming ran over schedule and Brown wasn't at training camp for the 1966 season, the team issued an ultimatum. Always one to go his own way, Brown shocked the sports world by retiring.

At the time of his retirement, Jim Brown was just thirty years old and still at the top of his game. He had gained a record 12,312 yards on 2,359 carries, averaging an amazing 5.2 yards every time he lugged the football. But once he left the game, he never looked back, going on to a solid movie career and later doing admirable work with troubled youths. When he retired, Jim Brown was considered the greatest runner of all time. Now, some forty years later with a ton of outstanding

LAST OF THE TWO-WAY PLAYERS

When veteran Chuck Bednarik made the final tackle in the 1960 championship game with the Packers, the Eagles' defensive star completed an incredible game. Bednarik had played both center and linebacker during his successful career, and while he started the season as the team's center, injuries necessitated him moving to linebacker. In the title game, the Eagles' coaching staff needed a tough veteran at each position and asked Bednarik to man both spots.

It must have looked strange to fans accustomed to seeing the defensive and offensive units change. Eleven Packers would leave the field at the switch, but just ten Eagles. Standing on the field alone was the 35-year-old Bednarik, waiting for his offensive, then defensive, teammates. He would end up playing the full sixty minutes, never leaving the field, in a throwback to football's earlier days. He was the last of the two-way players to go all the way, and after Philadelphia claimed the title, thanks to Bednarik's game-saving tackle, he promptly retired. And got some well-earned rest.

running backs having played since, Brown is still widely acclaimed as the greatest running back ever. That's how good he was.

The same year that Jim Brown retired, the Chicago Bears unveiled a rookie out of Kansas, a running back named Gale Sayers. Whereas Brown was speed and power, Sayers was speed, grace, and plenty of flash. He could fake, change directions in the blink of an eye, and accelerate very quickly in a way that left tacklers sprawling in his wake. George Halas and the Bears used him mainly on kickoff and punt returns for the first couple of games; then they made him a full-time running back. He turned into a veritable touchdown machine, and by the time the Bears faced the San Francisco 49ers in the twelfth game of the season, Sayers had scored sixteen touchdowns, just four short of the then-record held by Baltimore's Lenny Moore.

Gale Sayers would lead the NFL in rushing twice, in 1966 and 1969. The second title was more impressive because he had to come back from a very serious knee injury. However, a second knee injury would ultimately end his career prematurely. But while he was at the top of his game, Gale Sayers showed the NFL another dimension: the all-purpose runner who had the ability to score on any play and from any place on the field.

That same year, Sayers had a rookie teammate who put fear in the hearts of ball carriers everywhere. He was middle linebacker Dick Butkus, a 6'3", 250-pound giant whose game was hit, hit, and hit. Butkus was a one-man wrecking crew in the middle of the field who hit so hard, it hurt. He was the prototype for the big, strong linebackers who followed.

As terrific as Sayers and Butkus were, they were not the most notable rookies coming into pro football in 1965. There was yet another rookie, a quarterback, whose ascension to the pros would help change the entire shape of the game. His name was Joe Namath, and he had spent three seasons under Bear Byrant at the University of Alabama, setting numerous passing records and becoming an All-American. Though limited by a knee injury in 1964, the 6'2", 190-pound Namath showed his stuff to the country in the 1965 Orange Bowl game.

The University of Alabama's Crimson Tide was playing against the Texas Longhorns, with Namath on the bench. But when the Longhorns took the lead, Namath was pressed into duty with his knee heavily taped and braced. All he did was complete eighteen passes for 255 yards and two touchdowns, and though Texas won the game 21-17, the Alabama signal caller was chosen the Most Valuable Player. He had toughness, poise, presence, and a riflelike arm, qualities that made pro scouts drool. When the college draft rolled around, Namath became the top pick of both the NFL St. Louis Cardinals and AFL New York Jets. Then the bidding began.

In 1963, Jim Brown was reportedly the highest-paid player in football with a salary of $45,000 a year. When the bidding for Joe Namath ended less than two years later, the New York Jets signed him in 1965 to an unheard of contract worth $427,000. Namath liked the fact that Jets' owner Sonny Werblin had a show-business background and knew how to promote. And, sure enough, Namath became not only the most well-known rookie in the league but one of sports' most recognizable personalities, as well.

Namath quickly showed he was all player. He had a very strong arm and a quick release. The Jets didn't have a

Chicago Bears halfback Gale Sayers was one of football's most electrifying open-field runners. Though his career was shortened by knee injuries, those who saw Sayers say there was never another runner quite like him.

THE KANSAS COMET DAZZLES THE PRO FOOTBALL WORLD

When the Bears met the 49ers in a December game at a muddy and soggy Wrigley Field, no one was prepared for the brilliance of Gale Sayers. The 49ers had buried the Bears, 52-24, earlier in the season and looked to do it again. But while most of the players were slowed by the muddy field, Sayers just seemed to glide, cutting and reversing his field without losing a step. Early in the game he grabbed a short screen pass and promptly turned it into an 80-yard touchdown run, breaking through a host of defenders and then bursting to the goal line. That was just the beginning.

After that he scored four more times from scrimmage, going both long and short. His runs were of twenty-one, seven, fifty, and one yard. But he still wasn't finished. Late in the game he fielded a punt at his own 15-yard line and started upfield again. He zigged and zagged, faked and sprinted, and finally crossed the goal line after an 85-yard return. When it ended, the Bears had won the game 61-20, and Sayers had tied a record by scoring six touchdowns. In doing so, he had gained an incredible 336 all-purpose yards, broke the season touchdown record by running his total to twenty-two, and was quickly anointed as pro football's next great runner.

standout team, but they were getting better and now had the quarterback to lead them. In just a few short years, the entire sports world would know about Joe Namath and the New York Jets.

But Namath's contract did something else. It was a foreshadowing of a spending spree that crested early in 1966

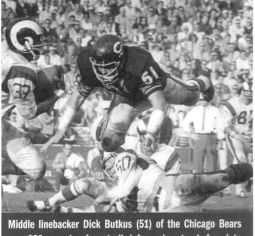

Middle linebacker Dick Butkus (51) of the Chicago Bears was 250 pounds of controlled fury who struck fear into opposing players for years.

when the rival leagues spent a combined $7 million to sign their draft choices. Of the 111 common draft choices, the older league inked seventy-nine, while the upstart AFL signed twenty-eight. It was time to do something, and do it quickly. The AFL was looking stronger every year and was obviously not going away.

One Big National Football League

It began with a series of secret meetings in the spring of 1966 between Lamar Hunt of the AFL Kansas City Chiefs and Tex Schramm of the NFL Dallas Cowboys. By June, NFL Commissioner Pete Rozelle shocked the football world by announcing a pending merger between the two leagues. Unlike the merger with the All-America Football Conference in 1950, the NFL would not simply be taking in a few teams. They would absorb the entire American Football League to form one big National Football League with twenty-four teams and plans to expand to twenty-eight by 1970.

Under the agreement, the AFL would retain its identity until the 1970 season, when the leagues would become one with a National and American Conference. But a common draft would begin immediately to end the bidding war, and, in January of 1967, there would be the first ever AFL-NFL World Championship Game. Several years later, this game would forever be known as the Super Bowl and become one of the most popular and watched events in all of sports.

On to the Super Bowl

Once the merger and the championship game were announced, the 1966 season became special. For the NFL, there was a lot of pride at stake. Old-timers remembered what had happened when the Cleveland Browns joined the league in 1950 and ended up champs. As for the younger league, they really had nothing to lose. If they were beaten, well, everyone expected it. But if their representative managed to win, that would be huge.

When the smoke cleared, the aging Green Bay Packers stood atop the NFL. The Pack finished 12-2 in the regular season and then defeated the young Dallas Cowboys, 34-27, to win the title. In the AFL it was the Kansas City Chiefs coming out on top. The Chiefs, under Coach Hank Stram, were 11-2-1 in the regular season, then rolled over the Buffalo Bills, 31-7, to earn their way to the big game.

The first-ever Super Bowl (as it is now known, though the name wasn't officially adopted until the fourth AFL-NFL title game) was held on January 15, 1967, at the Los Angeles Memorial Coliseum before 61,946 fans. The game was televised on both NBC and CBS, giving it a

Quarterback Joe Namath of the New York Jets made history when he signed a $427,000 contract with the New York Jets in 1965. Four years later he made history again when he led the Jets to victory over the Colts in Super Bowl III.

huge television audience. Kansas City had a fine quarterback in Len Dawson, a tough running back in Mike Garrett, and a breakaway wide receiver in Otis Taylor. They also had a lot of size on both the offensive and defensive lines, as well as a trio of tough linebackers and a solid defensive backfield.

The game was close for the first half. The wily Bart Starr had the Packers out in front early with a 37-yard TD pass to another vet, Max McGee. But K.C. came back, and by halftime Green Bay had just a 14-10 lead. Unbelievably, it was still anyone's game. That's when the Chiefs made some new-kid-on-the-block mistakes. Willie Wood intercepted a Len Dawson pass early in the third quarter and took it all the way to K.C.'s 5-yard line. Elijah Pitts then ran it in, and the rout was on. Green Bay dominated the rest of the way and won the first-ever Super Bowl 35-10.

A year later the Packers were back. First they defeated Dallas for the NFL title in 13-degrees-below-zero weather in Green Bay, when Bart Starr scored in the final seconds on a quarterback sneak. Then they met the Oakland Raiders in Super Bowl II in front of 75,546 fans at the Orange Bowl in Miami. This time the Packers simply dominated from beginning to end, leading 16-7 at the half and winning 33-14. In the eyes of most, Lombardi's troops had proven NFL superiority once and for all.

I remember that one well because I had joined the Raiders as an assistant coach under John Rauch in 1967. We were 13-1 that year and had an outstanding team. I couldn't have come into pro football in a better place, working under Rauch and team owner Al Davis, one of the great football minds of our time and a guy who wanted to win as much

Packers quarterback Bart Starr sets to pass in the Super Bowl I.

as I did. The Packers, of course, were legendary, but the AFL was playing top-notch football at that time and I loved the wide-open style of game we played. It never hurts coming to a winner, and the Raiders had talented players at almost every position. In fact, I thought then that the top teams in the AFL were equal to any the NFL had to offer.

It's funny, but the AFL-NFL title game wasn't even called the Super Bowl then, and to me it was like a college bowl game. You win your conference and go to a bowl game. Our reward for winning the AFL championship was to go to Miami and play the Green Bay Packers. Back then I simply didn't have any idea what this game would eventually become.

After Super Bowl II, Vince Lombardi resigned as head coach of the Packers. Green Bay had been close to being a dynasty in the 1960s, and names like Bart Starr, Jim Taylor, Paul Hornung, Boyd Dowler, Forrest

Gregg, Jerry Kramer, Willie Davis, Henry Jordan, Dave Robinson, Ray Nitschke, Herb Adderley, and Willie Wood are still remembered today, with many of them residing in Pro Football's Hall of Fame.

Namath's Guarantee

With the Packers fading because of age, there would be a new NFL champ in 1968. Many thought it would be the Dallas Cowboys, a team that finished at 12-2. But instead the Baltimore Colts emerged under Don Shula and wound up the regular season at 13-1. John Unitas was still there but had an injured elbow much of the year, and the team flourished under the veteran QB Earl Morrall.

There was also new power emerging in the AFL, one that football fans were watching carefully. It was the charismatic Joe Namath and the New York Jets. Namath had become a fine passer, though he sometimes threw both touchdowns and interceptions in bunches. But he had a deep-threat receiver in Don Maynard, a fine possession receiver in George Sauer, and two very solid running backs in Matt Snell and Emerson Boozer. In addition, the team had built a smart offensive line and a quick, opportunistic defense. The Jets finished the regular season at 11-3. In the AFL West, the Chiefs and Raiders both finished at 12-2, with the Raiders rolling in the playoff game, 41-6. When the Jets beat the Raiders 27-23 and the Colts whipped the Cleveland Browns 34-0 Super Bowl III was set.

Not too many fans felt the New Yorkers had a chance, especially when the Colts were made 17-point favorites to win the game. But the Jets didn't accept the company line. They felt they could stop the Colts and that the older Baltimore players would wilt in the Miami heat. They also felt that AFL quarterbacks played a different kind of game than their NFL counterparts, and that Namath could throw deep and also throw a quick out pass to the sideline better than any QB in the NFL. Then, three days

LOMBARDI

Vince Lombardi was my idol. It's as pure and simple as that. When I was a young coach I studied everything he did. When I was a junior college coach I went to a football clinic in Reno, Nevada, where he was speaking. I thought then I knew everything about coaching. That day, Lombardi spoke for eight hours...about one play: the Green Bay sweep. That's when I realized that my knowledge of coaching was superficial. I learned about real depth that day, about how much knowledge goes into what can seem the simplest of things. When Lombardi took over the Packers, he went back to basics, started from the very beginning, and built from there—step by step. He was truly an incredible coach.

before the game, Namath appeared before the Miami Touchdown Club and brashly told his audience, "The Jets will win on Sunday. I guarantee it."

His words made headlines. Both teams thought they would win, and when it was time to play, the New Yorkers delivered. Neither team scored in the first period, surprisingly. The Colts had more chances but were making mistakes. They missed a short field goal and had two Morrall passes intercepted. Then in the second period the Jets drove downfield, mixing off-tackle running plays by Snell with some sharp Namath passes to Sauer. Finally, Snell ran it in from the four, and the Jets took a 7-0 lead, which they still held at halftime.

Two Jim Turner field goals highlighted the third quarter and raised the Jets' lead to 13-0. Finally, in the fourth quarter, the Colts turned to the sore-elbowed Unitas. The Jets took a 16-0 lead before Unitas finally managed to get the Colts on the scoreboard. But that was as far as they got. The Jets won it 16-7, giving the AFL a victory in one of the great upsets in pro football history.

Namath had completed seventeen of twenty-eight passes for 206 yards, picking his spots and connecting when he had to. Fullback Snell set a then-Super Bowl record by rushing for 121 yards on thirty carries, while the Jets' secondary intercepted four Baltimore passes. It turned out to be a victory not only for the Jets and the AFL, but for all of football. The NFL was on the verge of being bigger and better, ready to enter another period of growth in which the sport would become more popular than ever.

Jets fullback Matt Snell follows a block by halfback Bill Mathis (31) to rip off a good gain against the Baltimore Colts in Super Bowl III. Snell gained a then-Super Bowl record 121 yards in the Jets' 16-7 upset victory.

Kansas City Chiefs coach Hank Stramm leads the cheers as his team defeats the Minnesota Vikings in Super Bowl IV. The victory gave AFL teams a 2-2 tie with the NFL in the four Super Bowl contests held before the leagues completed their full merger.

CHAPTER 6

Full Merger & the March to the Modern Game

Following the 1969 season, the two leagues had not only become more equal but were now fully merged. When the Kansas City Chiefs beat the Minnesota Vikings 23-7 in Super Bowl IV, it marked the last game between a separate American Football League and the NFL. Green Bay had won two for the NFL, while the Jets and Chiefs had pulled the AFL even. Now there would be just the American and National Conferences within a bigger-than-ever National Football League. Both conferences had three divisions—Eastern, Central, and Western—giving the expanded league six divisions and twenty-six teams.

Before the start of the 1969 season, I became the head coach of the Oakland Raiders. The Raiders were an AFL original, beginning play in 1960. When I took over from John Rauch, there was an expectation of excellence under owner Al Davis, who has a brilliant football mind. The team had won the AFL title in 1967 with a 13-1 regular season mark and a win over Houston before losing to the Packers in Super Bowl II. They were 12-2 the following year, losing to the Jets for the league championship, and then 12-1-1 my first year at the helm. We were beaten by Kansas City 17-7 for the AFL title, and they went on to win the Super Bowl.

The Raiders could strike fast through the air with Daryle Lamonica throwing to Warren Wells and Fred Biletnikoff. They had a big, fast offensive line with Gene Upshaw, Jim Otto, and Art Shell, and a punishing defense led by Ben Davidson, Ike Lassiter, Willie Brown, and Dave Grayson, just to name a few. I knew I had an outstanding team, and my job was to keep them on top and get them back to the Super Bowl.

In 1969, the legendary Vince Lombardi decided to coach again, taking over the Washington Redskins and immediately turning the team around, bringing them from 5-9 in 1968 to 7-5-2 in 1969. But shortly after the season ended, it was learned that Lombardi was suffering from cancer. He died at the age of fifty-seven on September 2, 1970. He was a great, great coach, and his death was a tremendous loss for football. Just a week later the NFL announced that the Super Bowl trophy would be renamed the Vince Lombardi Trophy in his honor.

On the field, the first year of the merger was successful. The Raiders slipped to 8-4-2 but still won the AFC West. We wound up in the title game against the Baltimore Colts, one of the original NFL teams that had been put into the AFC. The game turned out to be a battle of old quarterbacks. Daryle Lamonica was hurt early, and I had to put forty-three-year-old George Blanda into the game. The Colts still

AL DAVIS

Al Davis was the guy who gave me the opportunity to be a head coach in the NFL and had a tremendous influence on my life and career. I first met him when I was coaching at San Diego State. He was down there supposedly to scout and he began chatting with me about our defense. Later, I found out that was really a job interview, and I was hired to coach the Oakland Raiders linebackers under John Rauch. When Rauch left to become head coach of the Buffalo Bills, Al told the assistants they would all have jobs and he would talk to any of us about being the head coach. Even though I was just 32 years old, I told him I wanted the job. I figured I can either do it or I can't. After a couple of talks he gave me the chance and I coached there for 10 years. Al was a real innovator. He coached for three years, then became Commissioner of the AFL. It was his idea for the new league to go after the best quarterbacks, and his plan eventually led to the merger. Then he returned to the Raiders once more and continued to run a very successful organization.

Miami Dolphins Super Bowl ring 1972

had quarterback John Unitas, who was thirty-seven. It was 10-0 Baltimore when Blanda came in the game. The veteran made a valiant effort, but two of his late passes were picked off and Baltimore beat us 27-17. The Colts went on to win the Super Bowl 16-13 over the Dallas Cowboys. QB Earl Morrall relieved an injured Unitas and helped his club avenge their loss to the Jets in Super Bowl III.

The early 1970s saw more teams moving into new and modern stadiums, helping to expand the fan base even more. In 1970, the Steelers began playing in Three Rivers Stadium, while the Bengals moved into their new home, Riverfront Stadium in Cincinnati. The following year the Boston Patriots not only changed their name to the New England Patriots but also moved into Schaefer Stadium. The Eagles left old Franklin Field for Veterans Stadium, while the San Francisco 49ers settled into Candlestick Park, and the Dallas Cowboys left the Cotton Bowl for the brand-new Texas Stadium. All these stadiums were fan-friendly and geared to make the game more enjoyable for everyone. Several years earlier, in 1968, the Houston Oilers became the first team to play in a domed, indoor stadium when they moved into the Astrodome.

Dolphins fullback Larry Csonka was like a human battering ram when he had the football. Here he gains some of his record 145 yards against Minnesota in Super Bowl VIII, won by Miami, 24-7.

While the stadiums were improved, the players did have a complaint. Many of the new stadiums had artificial turf on the playing surface, making the players feel as if they were playing on carpet. This surface also spawned new kinds of injuries such as "turf toe," and the old-timers would simply say this ain't the way football was supposed to be played. This problem continued to plague players until newer stadiums returned to grass fields and technology allowed for a better, more grasslike turf in places where natural grass wasn't suitable.

On the field, a small number of teams dominated the decade, starting with the Miami Dolphins. Coached by Don Shula, the AFC Dolphins lost Super Bowl VI to the Dallas Cowboys, 24-3, following the 1971 season. But for the next two campaigns they were as close to perfect as any team could be. In fact, in 1972, the Dolphins *were* perfect.

The team went 14-0 in the regular season, then they swept through the playoffs to defeat George Allen's Washington Redskins in Super Bowl VII, 14-7, giving them a 17-0 season. This made them the first and only team in NFL history to go through both the regular and postseason with a perfect record. A year later they were 12-2 in the regular season and went on to whip the Minnesota Vikings 24-7 in Super Bowl VIII.

How did the Dolphins do it? They played a very controlled, economic game. They threw only when necessary, preferring to get the job done the old-fashioned way with a grind-it-out running attack and a defense that yielded very little. The Dolphins played as a team, in every sense of the word. They had a very efficient quarterback in Bob Griese, and three outstanding running backs, all of whom brought a different dimension to the game. Larry Csonka was a bone-crushing fullback who was also a 1,000-yard-plus rusher. The speedy Eugene "Mercury" Morris also gained 1,000 yards in 1972 and was capable of breaking away for long gains. Steady Jim Kiick was a good runner and fine receiver out of the backfield. In Paul Warfield, the club had a great pass receiver who could get open deep and also catch the ball in a crowd. The middle of the offensive line, with center Jim Langer and guards Bob Kuechenberg and Larry Little, was as good as it gets, and while veteran middle linebacker Nick Buoniconti was the most well-known defender, the entire the group gave up yards grudgingly.

The team's mettle was tested in their unbeaten season. Quarterback Griese was injured early, and Earl Mcrrall, who had filled in for John Unitas in Baltimore in 1968, was called upon again, and the team didn't miss a beat. Griese returned in the playoffs, and the team completed their perfect 17-0 season. In the Super Bowl, the Dolphins controlled the game with their economical style, Griese completing eight of just eleven passes for eighty-eight yards in the victory.

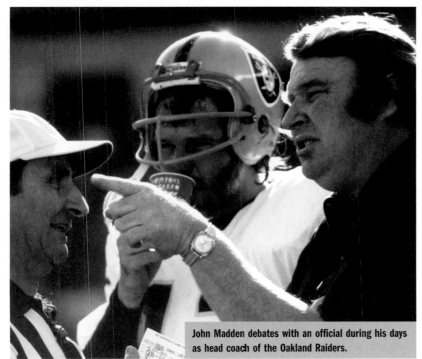

John Madden debates with an official during his days as head coach of the Oakland Raiders.

With more teams, more players, and more playoff games, the action on the field was hotter and heavier than ever. And in 1974, a new super team began rising near the banks of the Allegheny, Ohio, and Monongahela rivers. The Pittsburgh Steelers had been in the NFL since 1933 and had never won a title. Now in the AFC, the Steelers

O.J. RUNS FOR 2,000

A sensational running back with speed and moves, Orenthal James Simpson rose to fame in his two seasons at the University of Southern California. College football fans spent the 1967 and 1968 seasons asking the same question: "How many yards did O.J. get?" In 1968, Simpson won the Heisman Trophy and gained 1,309 yards. He was then drafted by the lowly AFL Buffalo Bills, and suddenly O.J. came down to earth. The Bills had an offensive line nicknamed "The Vanishing Five," and Simpson learned what it was like to be gang-tackled nearly every time he had the ball. In the eyes of fans who didn't know, O.J. was dubbed a disappointment.

But by 1973, the Bills had revamped their offensive line, which featured a pair of outstanding guards, Reggie McKenzie and Joe DeLamielleure. In the opener against New England, O.J. ran for a record 250 yards. And by the time the season ended, people were again asking "How many yards did O.J. get?" The answer was 2,003, on 332 carries, an average of six yards a pop. He became the first back to gain more than 2,000 yards in a season and went on to a stellar career in the NFL.

were an improving lot under Coach Chuck Noll. I experienced it firsthand in 1972 when I coached the Raiders to a 10-3-1 record to win the AFC West. The Steelers, at 11-3, took the AFC Central, and we ended up meeting in the first round of the playoffs. That was the year the Dolphins were 14-0 in the AFC East, so there were three great teams, and we all couldn't win the conference title.

The game was played at Three Rivers Stadium in Pittsburgh and was for the most part a defensive battle. It was scoreless at the half, and by the fourth quarter the Raiders were trailing 6-0 on a pair of field goals by Roy Gerela. With time running down, I decided to put

Strong-armed Terry Bradshaw joined a group of all-star players to make the Pittsburgh Steelers the best team of the 1970s. With Bradshaw at quarterback, the Steelers would win four Super Bowl titles during the decade.

my young quarterback, Ken "The Snake" Stabler, in the game to replace veteran Daryle Lamonica. Kenny led us downfield, and with just 1:13 left on the clock he broke out of the pocket and ran down the left sideline for a 30-yard score. The kick gave us a 7-6 lead. We felt we were in good shape until we became victims of one of the most unusual plays in football history.

Pittsburgh didn't have a lot of time, and with just twenty-two seconds left they were facing a fourth-and-ten at their own 40-yard line. All we had to do was stop them one more time. Quarterback Terry Bradshaw dropped straight back. Everyone was expecting a long pass downfield, so we rushed him hard and he had to scramble out of the pocket to his right. He then fired the ball over the middle in the direction of halfback John Fuqua, who was covered by my tough safety, Jack Tatum. Tatum, Fuqua, and the ball all came together at our 35-

ANOTHER NEW LEAGUE

The NFL had labor problems in 1974 with the players going on strike on July 1st. It would end in August, but by then a new rival league had started play. The World Football League (WFL) debuted with twelve teams in July and began to throw big money around, signing a number of respected NFL players to future contracts. Among them were Larry Csonka, Jim Kiick, and Paul Warfield, all of the two-time champion Dolphins.

Sure enough, the WFL made it through the first season with the Birmingham Americans defeating the Florida Blazers 22-21 in the first-ever World Bowl, their championship game. But another price war in pro football never happened. The league started its second season, but soon ran out of money and folded on October 22, 1975. The players ticketed for the WFL returned to their NFL teams.

yard line. Suddenly, the ball ricocheted off someone and flew backward. Many of the players stopped running, figuring it was an incomplete pass.

But fullback Franco Harris, who was trailing the play, grabbed the ball at his ankles before it hit the ground and took off down the left sideline. By the time the players realized there was no whistle, it was too late. Harris ran all the way to the end zone for an apparent touchdown. We protested. According to the rules then, a ball could not bounce off one receiver to another, and we thought it hit Fuqua.

The Steelers said it hit Tatum, and in pre-instant-replay days, the refs agreed. The catch was dubbed "The Immaculate Reception" and is still remembered as that today. All it did was cost us a shot at the Super Bowl.

Pittsburgh finally broke through in 1974, defeating Minnesota 16-6. The following year they did it again, whipping the Dallas Cowboys and their fine quarterback, Roger Staubach, 21-17 in a great game. Then came 1976, a year I'll never forget. The Oakland Raiders almost ran the table, finishing 13-1 in the regular season, with only a loss to New England keeping us from a perfect record. This was the season I felt the team could win it all. We were loaded with talent.

Steelers fullback Franco Harris on his way to a game-winning touchdown after making "The Immaculate Reception" on a pass from Terry Bradshaw in the AFC Divisional Playoff game against Oakland in December of 1972.

THE 4-3 DEFENSE

The basic 4-3 NFL defense features four linemen, three linebackers, and four defensive backs. When defending against opponents expected to throw many forward passes, teams most often use the 4-3 formation. The positioning of the defensive players depends upon the offensive formation they're facing.

DE = Defensive End
DT = Defensive Tackle
OLB = Outside Linebacker
MLB = Middle Linebacker

C = Cornerback
SS = Strong Safety
FS = Free Safety

Ken Stabler was at the top of his game. A left-handed thrower, "The Snake" would complete 67 percent of his passes and throw for twenty-seven touchdowns. Fullback Mark Van Eaghen ran for more than 1,000 yards. Dave Casper, a 6'4" bruiser at tight end, caught fifty-three passes, while speedy Cliff Branch caught forty-six, but gained 1,111 yards for an average of twenty-four yards a catch. Veteran Fred Biletnikoff was still a strong third-down receiver, and the offensive line featured that great guard/tackle tandem on the left side, Gene Upshaw and Art Shell. The defense was also top-notch. John Matuszak and Otis Sistrunk anchored the line, Ted Hendricks and Phil Villapiano were stars at linebacker, and Butch Atkinson, Willie Brown, and Jack Tatum led the defensive backfield. We were a solid and deep team.

NO MORE "YEAH, BUT..."

One thing I learned over the years is that getting to the Super Bowl doesn't mean a thing. You have to win it. Beating the Vikings was the biggest thrill of my life, but it meant even more than that. I remember going to a banquet after we had won and one of the first guys to congratulate me was former Cowboys quarterback Roger Staubach. He said that by winning no one can ever again tell you that you couldn't do it. A lot of players and coaches have to live with that *Yeah, but,* as in *Yeah, but you couldn't win a championship*. It can be like a gorilla on your shoulders. It's happened with great players like Dan Marino and O.J. Simpson, and outstanding coaches like George Allen, Marv Levy, and Bud Grant. They all reached the Super Bowl...*Yeah, but*...Winning the Super Bowl eliminates all that, and it's something you'll always have.

Oakland Raiders quarterback Ken "The Snake" Stabler throws one of his left-handed passes in a 1977 rout of the Seattle Seahawks. Stabler was one of the Raiders players who helped John Madden's ball club win Super Bowl XI over the Minnesota Vikings in January of 1977.

In the playoffs, we had to come back with fourteen fourth-quarter points to beat New England 24-21, avenging our only loss of the year. Then we went up against Pittsburgh, which was 10-4 in the regular season. Both the Steelers' running backs—Franco Harris and Rocky Bleier—missed the game with injuries. We won it 24-7, but I'd like to think we would have beaten them even with their running backs healthy. It was our year. In Super Bowl XI we had to go up against the Minnesota Vikings and their elusive quarterback, Fran Tarkenton.

Like I said, it was the Oakland Raiders' year. We scored sixteen points in the second quarter and thirteen more in the fourth. Meanwhile, our defense did its job, and we won the game and the championship 32-14. Our halfback, Clarence Davis, ran for 137 yards, Biletnikoff caught four passes for seventy-nine yards, helping to set up three TDs, and cornerback Willie Brown returned an interception seventy-five yards for a score. For a coach, it was the greatest feeling in the world—all the hours, all the work, all the tension, and finishing it off with a championship. Needless to say, it's something I'll never forget. It's even more special today because we didn't win another one while I was there. I coached three more seasons and felt I was ready to move on. So it was off the sidelines and up to the broadcast booth.

The Steelers, however, weren't done. After a very good Dallas Cowboys team won Super Bowl XII over the Denver Broncos 27-10 in the first title game played at a domed stadium, the Louisiana Superdome, the Steelers rose to prominence once again. In 1978 and 1979 they went 14-2 and 12-4 in the regular season and both times captured the Super Bowl, first defeating Dallas 35-31 in another nail-biter, then the following year they topped the L.A. Rams 31-19, coming from behind with two fourth-quarter touch-downs. Not only were the Steelers the first team to win the Super Bowl three times, but they had now won it on four occasions. As the Green Bay Packers dominated the 1960s, it was the Pittsburgh Steelers that became the team of the 1970s.

What Made the Steelers Great?

Chuck Noll had put together a well-balanced team. Offensively, they could run and pass effectively. Quarterback Terry Bradshaw had one of the best arms in the game and had not one but two explosive wide receivers in Lynn Swann and John Stallworth. Fullback Franco Harris was a perennial 1,000-yard runner and one of the best ever. Rocky Bleier, who overcame serious leg wounds suffered while serving in Vietnam, became a reliable runner, great blocker, and good pass receiver out of the backfield.

The rebuilding began in 1970. Coach Noll had a 1-13 team his first season of 1969 and the next year made 6'4", 270-pound defensive tackle "Mean" Joe Greene the team's number-one draft choice. The

Defensive tackle "Mean" Joe Greene (75) anchored the Steel Curtain defense of the championship Pittsburgh Steelers teams of the 1970s.

club also acquired Terry Bradshaw that season and built from there. While the Steelers worked to build their defense, they didn't ignore the offense, either. The offensive line was anchored by center Mike Webster, guard Sam Davis, and tackle Jon Kolb. As for the defense, they seemed to have stars everywhere.

Greene was joined on the line by ends L.C. Greenwood and Dwight White and tackles Ernie Holmes and Steve Furness. Middle linebacker Jack Lambert was an inspiration, a player who put it all on the line every week, tough as he was skilled; and outside linebacker Jack Ham was a perennial All-Pro, an all-time great, a tough, smart, and opportunistic defender. Defensive back Mel Blount was another top star, as were backfield mates Donnie Shell and Mike Wagner. This team was loaded with talent and, when firing on all cylinders, very tough to beat.

Dallas also had a terrific team throughout the 1970s, winning a pair of Super Bowls. But they had a very hard time defeating the Steelers. When the two teams met, it was always war. The Cowboys were also a star-studded crew. Roger Staubach, who came to the NFL after serving four years in the Navy, was one of the great clutch quarterbacks of all time. He had a breakaway runner in Tony Dorsett and a pair of outstanding receivers in Drew Pearson and Tony Hill. The team always featured an exceptional offensive line, with the stars in the late 1970s being tackle Rayfield Wright, center John Fitzgerald, and guard Herbert Scott. The defense was absolutely stellar. Ed "Too Tall" Jones was a 6'8" behemoth at defensive end, and running mate

LOST IDENTITIES

In the early 1960s, the Giants had Jim Katcavage and Andy Robustelli at defensive ends, and John Lovetere and Dick Modzelewski at tackles. The press and the fans began referring to them as "Ko, Lo, Mo, Ro," a play on their last names. This was the beginning of nicknames for defensive lines. Before long, the Minnesota Vikings' defensive line became "The Purple People Eaters," with Jim Marshall and Carl Eller at ends, and Alan Page and Gary Larson at tackles. The Rams featured "The Fearsome Foursome," with Deacon Jones and Lamar Lundy at ends, and Merlin Olsen and Roger Brown at tackles, while the Steelers had the dreaded "Steel Curtain," with Dwight White and L.C. Greenwood at ends, and Joe Greene and Ernie Holmes at tackles. These names stuck, even when some of the personnel changed. But in those days the guys often stayed together for years, learned each other's moves, worked together as a unit, and blended their individual talents into one. The players today are still great, but they switch teams so often that there's no time for a unit to acquire a nickname based on the individual styles and personalities of the players.

Harvey Martin was an All-Pro. Tackle Randy White was an all-time great, and 6'6" Jethro Pugh was tough to move out of the middle. The linebackers were solid, if not spectacular, and the defensive backfield featured standout players in safeties Cliff Harris and Charlie Waters,

and a few years earlier, cornerback Mel Renfro. This was another very impressive team under Coach Tom Landry, but the Steelers were just a little stronger.

Rule Changes and Other Developments

During this period of continued growth and expansion, the game continued to change and evolve. Let's take a look at some of the most important developments of this period that ended in 1980.

• The inbounds lines, or hash marks, were moved even farther toward the center of the field in 1972. They were now 23 yards, 1 foot, and 9 inches from the sidelines, a big difference from the ten yards in 1933.

• In 1973, a jersey-numbering system was adopted. Now, quarterbacks and kicking specialists had to wear numbers between 1 and 19; running backs and defensive backs, 20–49; centers and linebackers, 50–59; defensive linemen and interior offensive linemen other than the center, 60–79; and wide receivers and tight ends, 80–89. Players already in the NFL at the time of the change could continue to use their old numbers.

• In 1974, one sudden-death overtime period was added for preseason and regular-season games. No one liked tie games, and this rule made them increasingly rare. Also, on missed field goals from beyond the 20-yard line, the ball would be given to the defensive team at the line of scrimmage, not at the 20-yard line, which had previously been automatic.

• That same year, the goalposts were moved from the goal line to the end lines, making field goals a bit more difficult, and kickoffs now originated from the 35-yard line instead of the 40-yard line.

• The Seattle Seahawks would become another expansion team, beginning play in 1976.

PAYTON RUNS FOR 275 YARDS

Walter Payton, a 5'11", 200-pound running back, joined the Chicago Bears out of tiny Jackson State University in 1975. Payton gained just 679 yards as a rookie, and few felt he was ticketed for greatness. A year later, however, he erupted for 1,390 yards on 311 carries and had arrived as a star. But this was just the beginning. In 1977, Payton led the league with 1,852 rushing yards on 339 carries. In a November 20th game against Minnesota, the man who would become known as "Sweetness" erupted for a record 275 yards on forty carries and helped the Bears to their first winning season in ten years. That season he would also become the NFL's youngest-ever Most Valuable Player. When he finally retired he was the league's all-time leading rusher, a mark since broken in 2002 by Emmitt Smith. But Payton was a dedicated runner who trained ferociously, had amazing acceleration, and worked for every last yard he gained.

Chicago Bears Hall of Fame running back Walter Payton was a relentless ball carrier year after year and retired as the NFL's all-time leader rusher, until his record was finally broken by Emmitt Smith.

• More domed stadiums opened. In 1975, the Detroit Lions got out of the unpredictable Midwestern weather by moving to the Pontiac (Michigan) Silverdome, and the New Orleans Saints moved into the Louisiana Superdome.

• In 1978, the schedule was increased from fourteen to sixteen regular-season games. The old twelve-game schedule must have seemed like a cakewalk to players going sixteen.

• More rule changes favored the offense. In 1977, the head slap by defensive linemen was outlawed, and defenders were only allowed to make contact with eligible receivers once. Offensive linemen were now prohibited from thrusting their hands at an opponent's neck, face, or head.

• The Dallas Cowboys' victory over the Denver Broncos in Super Bowl XII on January 15, 1978, was watched by more than 102 million people, making it the most watched show in the history of television. No more disputing the popularity of the game.

• In 1978, a rule change prohibited defenders from maintaining contact with a receiver except for within five yards of the line of scrimmage. There was restricted contact after that in yet another attempt to open up the offense.

• To ensure more player safety, a 1979 rule prohibited players on the receiving team from blocking below the waist during kickoffs, punts, and field goal attempts.

There was no doubt anymore about the longevity of the National Football League. By 1980, many felt professional football had surpassed Major League Baseball as the country's most popular spectator sport. It was also big business with more teams, new stadiums, and more television money, a colorful spectacle being played out week after week. Needless to say, there was still much more to come.

Quarterback Dan Fouts (14) of the San Diego Chargers lets a pass fly in a 1981 game against Tampa Bay. Fouts keyed a devastating, wide-open passing attack tabbed "Air Coryell," after the Chargers coach and architect of the offense, Don Coryell.

CHAPTER 7

Montana, Walsh & the West Coast Offense

1980-1990

The beginning of the 1980s marked the changing of the guard in the NFL, at least to some degree. A couple of the top teams from the 1970s, notably the Steelers and Dolphins, were in need of some rebuilding. Others, like the Cowboys and Raiders, were still close to the top of their game, and several new teams, such as the Philadelphia Eagles and San Diego Chargers, were beginning to make their presence felt.

In 1980, a number of teams compiled fine records without having the usual bevy of superstar performers. In the NFC, for example, the Philadelphia Eagles under Coach Dick Vermeil finished at 12-4 without a 1,000-yard rusher or pass receiver, and with Ron Jaworski, a quarterback who had to keep proving himself every year despite his success. And in the AFC, the San Diego Chargers were bringing something different to the game.

Originally an AFL entry with an explosive attack in the early 1960s, the Chargers had rebuilt under Coach Don Coryell and were once again playing all-out, wide-open football. With a quick-release quarterback in Dan Fouts and an incredible trio of receivers in wideouts John Jefferson and Charlie Joiner and tight end Kellen Winslow, the team became known as "Air Coryell" for its aggressive passing attack and won the AFC West at 11-5. Fouts threw for 4,715 yards, and the top three receivers all had more than 1,000 yards catching passes. Yet at the outset of the 1980 playoffs, there was no obviously clear-cut favorite.

When the smoke cleared there was another first. The Oakland Raiders, my old ball club, became the first wild-card playoff entry to win the Super Bowl. The Raiders, now coached by former quarterback Tom Flores, first beat the Houston Oilers 27-7, then held off San Diego in a real shootout, 34-27, and finally topped Philadelphia in

Super Bowl XV, 27-10. Though a lot of teams were playing well that season, the Raiders were as good as anyone.

In 1981, another team was on the rise, and this was one that wouldn't go away quickly. When Bill Walsh took over the San Francisco 49ers in 1979, he was inheriting a team that had just come off a terrible, 2-14 season. With Walsh at the helm, the 'Niners promptly finished 2-14 once

THE TYLER ROSE

Earl Campbell, the Houston Oilers' running back from Tyler, Texas, was one of the great runners of his time. He joined the Oilers out of the University of Texas in 1978 and led the NFL in rushing in each of his first three seasons. Campbell was a 5'11", 244-pound bruiser with 36-inch thighs. He was a punishing runner with speed to burn, and defenders took a beating trying to bring him down. During his third season, in 1980, he set an NFL record, running for more than 200 yards in four different games, and he finished the season with 1,934 yards, at the time the second-best single-season rushing performance in history.

Gradually, the beating he took week after week wore him down, and he retired after the 1985 season with 9,407 yards and seventy-four rushing touchdowns. Because he never played in a Super Bowl and didn't have a long career, it's easy to forget him now, but Earl Campbell was one of the best. And because Tyler, Texas, is known for its rose-growing industry, this bruising running back had the rather unusual nickname of "The Tyler Rose."

again. San Francisco was quarterbacked by journeyman Steve DeBerg that year, while a rookie out of Notre Dame named Joe Montana played sparingly, throwing just twenty-three passes. As good as he had been at Notre Dame, most pro scouts felt Montana didn't have a big-league arm, and because of that he wasn't a high draft pick.

Bill Walsh made sure the defense was well served, but it was the offense that began turning heads. The 'Niners didn't have the luxury of a standout running back in 1981, so Walsh devised a passing attack built around Montana. The wide receivers were Dwight Clark, who wasn't that fast but always seemed to be open, and speedy Freddie Solomon, who could really motor after he caught the ball. Tight end Charlie Young was a former All-Pro, while fullback Earl Cooper was an outstanding receiver out of the backfield. They were all tools for Joe Montana.

The original knock on Montana when he left Notre Dame was true: He didn't have a cannon for a throwing arm. But Montana was a leader, a resourceful quarterback who was extremely cool under pressure. He had the ability to play his best when his team needed him the most, and he was an extremely accurate passer. The offense built around Montana's talents came to be known as the "West Coast Offense."

By throwing a variety of short and medium-length passes, Montana and his receivers would move the ball downfield with only minimal help from the running game. Unlike the quarterbacks from an earlier generation, Montana rarely cranked up and whistled the ball far

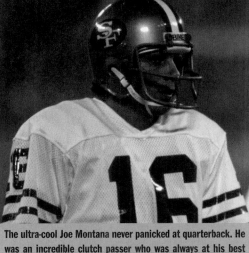

The ultra-cool Joe Montana never panicked at quarterback. He was an incredible clutch passer who was always at his best when the game was on the line. He led the San Francisco 49ers to four Super Bowl triumphs and is considered by many the greatest of all time.

downfield. His passing offense was controlled and calculated, as low-risk as a passing attack could be. And it worked beautifully. After losing two of their first three games, the 'Niners won twelve of the next thirteen to finish the year at a surprising 13-3. Montana had completed 311 of 488 passes for 3,565 yards and nineteen touchdowns.

Then the young quarterback gave the football world a full look at his talents in the NFC championship game against the Dallas Cowboys at Candlestick Park in San Francisco. In a back-and-forth game, Dallas finally took a 27-21 lead in the fourth quarter. When the 'Niners got the ball at their own 11-yard line there was just 4:54 left. Montana steadily moved his team upfield, using running plays to offset the Cowboys prevent-defense, designed to stop the pass. Finally, with fifty-eight seconds left, the ball was at the Dallas 6-yard line and the 'Niners had a third-and-three.

Montana took the snap and dropped straight back. He looked for Freddie Solomon in the left corner of the end zone. Not only was Solomon covered, but defensive end Ed "Too Tall" Jones and his 6'8" frame was bearing down on the QB. Montana coolly scrambled to his right, and as he neared the sideline, he lofted a pass deep in the end zone. There was Dwight Clark, just in front of the end line, leaping high in the air and grabbing the ball at the top of his jump for the winning touchdown. The play would forever go down in the annals of 49ers football simply as "The Throw" and "The Catch."

Two weeks later the 'Niners won Super Bowl XVI with a 26-21 victory over the Cincinnati Bengals at the Pontiac Silverdome. Some thought

THE NFL BECOMES MORE POPULAR THAN EVER

By 1981, there was increasing evidence that the National Football League was bigger than ever. At one point during the season a CBS-*New York Times* poll showed that 48 percent of sports fans preferred football to 31 percent for baseball. Then, after the season, it was announced that regular-season attendance had reached 13.6 million, an average of 60,745 fans per game. It was a new record for the fourth year in a row and the first time the per-game average topped the 60,000 mark. In fact, all NFL games that year were played before 93.8 percent of total stadium capacity. Finally, Super Bowl XVI had the highest rating of any televised sporting event ever. The game was watched by a record 110.2 million fans, with an additional record 14 million listening over the radio.

it was a fluke, and that San Francisco and Joe Montana would be one-year wonders. But they would soon prove they were a lot more than that.

Another players' strike in 1982 split the season and shortened it to nine games. At the end, a special Super Bowl Tournament was set up with sixteen teams participating. When this strange season ended, the Washington Redskins were the new champs with a 27-17 victory over Miami. A year later, with the schedule back to normal, the Raiders topped the Redskins 38-9 for their third Super Bowl triumph. Then, in 1984, the top two teams from both the NFC and AFC made it to the Super Bowl as the forward pass really took center stage.

Miami's Dan Marino was a pure passer who was a star from his first game as a rookie in 1983. Marino played his entire career with the Miami Dolphins and retired with almost all the major passing records under his belt.

During the regular season, second-year quarterback Dan Marino, out of the University of Pittsburgh, led the Miami Dolphins to a 14-2 record. The 6'4", 215-pound Marino was a drop-back passer with a quick release, and the Dolphins, under Don Shula, used his talents to develop a devastating passing game. The team's top rusher, Woody Bennett, gained just 606 yards, but the top pass receivers, Mark Clayton and Mark Duper, both caught passes for more than 1,300 yards. As for Marino, he was being touted as the game's next great passer. He completed 362 of 564 passes for a record 5,084 yards and an incredible forty-eight touchdowns, another new mark.

But the Dolphins didn't have the league's best record. That honor went to the San Francisco 49ers. The team had a more bal-

A SEASON OF RECORDS

Dan Marino's 5,084 passing yards and forty-eight touch-down tosses were only two of a whole series of great records set during the 1984 season. Running back Eric Dickerson of the Rams rushed for 2,105 yards, breaking the record set by O.J. Simpson in 1973, though Dickerson played a sixteen-game schedule to Simpson's fourteen. Art Monk of the Washington Redskins shook loose often enough to catch a record 106 passes, and Walter Payton, still picking up yards for the Bears, moved past the great Jim Brown as the NFL's all-time leading rusher. Payton finished the season with 13,309 yards...and counting.

anced offense now, with Wendell Tyler running for 1,262 yards and Roger Craig for 649. Joe Montana threw for 3,630 yards and twenty-eight touchdowns, well below Marino's numbers, but many still considered him the game's best. He led the 'Niners to a 15-1 regular-season mark, and it was only fitting that these two teams and two stellar quarterbacks meet for the championship.

Super Bowl XIX was played at Stanford (California) Stadium before 84,059 fans. Many felt that the 'Niners wouldn't be able to cope with Marino's passing and that the Dolphins' defense, known as the "Killer Bees" because nine of the eleven starters had last names beginning with the letter B, could stop the 'Niners. When Marino completed nine of his first ten passes for 103 yards and had the Dolphins out front 10-7 at the end of the first quarter, the new kid on the block seemed in charge. But as soon as the second period began, the momentum changed, and the 49ers began laying claim to being the team of the 1980s. Joe Montana once again proved there were few better when a big game was on the line.

Montana led his team to three second-period scores and a 28-16 halftime lead. The second half was more of the same as the 'Niners continued to use five defensive backs and turned defensive end Fred Dean loose to chase Marino. The strategy shut down the vaunted Miami passing attack, and the 'Niners rolled to a 38-16 victory to notch their second Super Bowl title.

Marino, who had to play from behind most of the way, wound up passing the football fifty times, completing twenty-nine for 318 yards. He threw for one score and was intercepted twice. Montana, on the other hand, completed twenty-four of thirty-five passes for 331 yards and three touchdowns. While fullback Roger Craig set a Super Bowl record by scoring three times, it was Joe Montana who was the runaway choice for the game's Most Valuable Player.

To me, Joe Montana is the best offensive player I've ever seen. There's nothing tougher than playing quarterback in the NFL, and Joe was close to perfect. All quarterbacks do essentially the same thing. They take a three-, five-, or seven-step drop, then look upfield, read the pattern, and deliver the ball. Some do it better than others and make it look easier. Joe did it better and made it look easier than anyone. He was simply a very tough guy who really knew how to play the game.

The Chicago Bears' fierce middle line-backer Mike Singletary (50) was the key to the team's devastating "46 Defense," which allowed the Bears to dominate the league and become champions in 1985.

More Outstanding Teams

Following their triumph over the Dolphins in Super Bowl XIX, the 49ers would remain among the NFL top teams, but it would be four years before they would return to the Super Bowl. In the intervening three years, three longstanding NFL teams, now in the NFC, would rise up to dominate the seasons of 1985, 1986, and 1987. They were the Chicago Bears, New York Giants, and Washington Redskins. Both the Bears and Giants would be nearly unbeatable, while the surprising Redskins, lacking star power at the so-called glamour positions, would upset a lot of apple carts on their way to the title.

The Chicago Bears had been coming on under Coach Mike Ditka, a former All-Pro tight end. The team won the NFC Central in 1984 with a 10-6 mark but lost in the playoffs. By 1985 they had put it all together. Quarterback Jim McMahon didn't have the greatest arm in the world and was injury prone. But when healthy, he was a confident leader who always found a way to get the job done. Walter Payton, at age thirty-one, was still good enough to gain 1,551 yards on 324 carries during the regular season. Wide receiver Willie Gault grabbed just thirty-three passes in a ball-control, run-oriented attack, but he averaged 21.3 yards a catch.

In the eyes of many, however, it was the defense that made the Bears so dangerous. There were outstanding players everywhere. The defensive line featured the pass rushing of Richard Dent, veteran tackles Dan Hampton and Steve McMichael, and a huge rookie named William "The Refrigerator" Perry. Mike Singletary was a mobile and tough middle linebacker, perhaps the key to the entire defense, while defensive backs Gary Fencik and Dave Duerson also did a fine job. Defensive coach Buddy Ryan brought his talented players together with a scheme called the "46 Defense."

The defense was named after a former Bears safety, Doug Plank, who wore number 46 and almost operated like an additional linebacker. The defense typically had six defenders on the line of scrimmage, put a lot of pressure on the quarterback, and smothered the running game. It all came together in 1985. The Bears were 15-1 in the regular season, leading the league in defense. Dent was on the top in sacks with seventeen, Fencik led the club with 118 tackles, and Singletary was named Defensive Player of the Year by several polls.

In the playoffs, the Bears' defense really rose to the occasion, shutting out first the Giants, 21-0, then the Rams, 24-0, in the NFC title game. Now it was on to Super Bowl XX, where the Bears would play the surprising New England Patriots, which had just become the first wild-card team to win three playoff games on the road, including a 31-14 upset of the Miami Dolphins for the AFC title. Still, few thought they could beat the Bears.

The experts were right. It was Chicago's day from the outset. They chased starting quarterback Tony Eason after he misfired on his first six passes, bringing veteran Steve Grogan into the game. It didn't help. McMahon and the offense rolled. The defense recovered a pair of fumbles early. And by the time the Bears left the field at halftime with a 23-3 lead, they had gained 236 total yards while the Pats had minus twelve. The final score was 46-10, and even Refrigerator Perry scored a touchdown on a 1-yard run from the fullback position. The Bears, and the 46 Defense, were champs.

A year later it was the New York Giants, another team that was marked by its strong defense. The Giants had been rebuilt by a relentless coach named Bill Parcells who would accept nothing less than the best from his players. If they couldn't handle Parcells' work ethic and sharp tongue, they were gone. Just like

L.T.

Lawrence Taylor was born in Williamsburg, Virginia, on February 4, 1959. Surprisingly, he didn't begin playing football until his junior year at Lafayette High School. From there it was on to an All-American career at the University of North Carolina, where Taylor terrorized quarterbacks, running backs, and anyone else who got in his way. The Giants made him the number-two overall pick in the 1981 draft and turned him loose. Taylor had 9.5 sacks as a rookie and became an instant All-Pro.

L.T., as he was called, was a dominant, innovative player

Known to almost everyone as "L.T.," New York Giants outside linebacker Lawrence Taylor was an impact player on defense from day one and is often called the most dominant defensive player ever. He was so good that he often single-handedly changed the flow of an entire game.

harm's way. He was a player to be feared all over the league for the way he could single-handedly disrupt an offense.

He did it by changing the way teams had to pass protect. The Giants played a three-man defensive line, and he was the open-side linebacker and he rushed almost all the time. Teams just didn't know how to block him. At first they tried a running back. Didn't work. Then Bill Walsh at San Francisco tried pulling a guard to block him with the tackle blocking the end. He beat that, too. There were times when he was virtually unstoppable. He was not only a great play-

from day one. He was 6'3" and 240 pounds of fury, fast as he was strong, reckless as he was cunning. In a sense, he was the ultimate playmaker. If you needed a sack, he got it. If a runner came his way looking for a first down, he'd stop him. L.T. seemed to have no regard for his body and was quick to put it in

er who made tackles and piled up sacks, but he changed the way offenses would protect the passer. He was a totally dominant player and in all my years in the broadcast booth the best defensive player I ever saw.

That's how good L.T. was.

that. Those who stayed knew the coach would make them winners and came to respect and admire him. In 1986, the team had a very competent quarterback in Phil Simms and a workhorse running back, Joe Morris, who would gain 1,516 yards. The team's best pass receiver was tough tight end Mark Bavaro, who would catch sixty-six passes for 1,001 yards. It was an adequate offense, not an explosive one.

The defense, however, turned heads. Nose tackle Jim Burt and defensive ends George Martin and Leonard Marshall were all impressive. The defensive backfield, with the likes of Mark Collins, Kenny Hill, and Terry Kinard, was solid. But it was the linebackers that struck fear into opponents. The starting quartet of Harry Carson, Carl Banks, Gary Reasons, and Lawrence Taylor were simply awesome. Carson and Banks would be multiple Pro Bowl selections and are considered franchise all-time greats. Taylor, however, was simply extra special, a player considered by many as the best ever at his position and a guy who could literally be a one-man wrecking crew.

In 1986, Parcells and his Taylor-led Giants completed the regular season with a 14-2 mark. Taylor finished with 20.5 sacks and was named the league's Most Valuable Player, the first defender to achieve that honor since Minnesota tackle Alan Page won it back in 1971.

The Giants then proceeded to whip through the playoffs. First they blasted Joe Montana and the 49ers, 49-3. Joe Morris ran for 159 yards, and L.T. intercepted a pass and took it thirty-four yards to the end zone. Next, the defense took over in the NFC title game against Washington, playing in gusty winds at Giants Stadium. The New Yorkers won 17-0 and advanced to Super Bowl XXI against the Denver Broncos and their strong-armed quarterback, John Elway. Elway had engineered a last-minute, 98-yard drive against Cleveland to tie the game, then led his

team to a victory in overtime. He was much like Joe Montana in that respect, but with a much stronger throwing arm.

In the Super Bowl, however, it was the Giants who showed their greatness. The Broncos had a 10-9 halftime lead, but in the second half, Phil Simms took over. The Giants quarterback would complete twenty-two of twenty-five passes for 268 yards and three touchdowns as New York went on to win, 39-20. The defense shut down the Denver running game, with linebacker Carl Banks leading the way with ten tackles. It was New York's year.

Joe Gibbs' Washington Redskins emerged from the pack in 1987 with an 11-4 regular-season record, then marched through the playoffs and stomped all over the Denver Broncos, 42-10, in Super Bowl XXII. Unheralded quarterback Doug Williams threw for 340 yards and led his club to a record thirty-five second-quarter points, and a rookie running back named Tim Smith ran for a Super Bowl record 204 yards.

It's a Gatorade shower for New York Giants coach Bill Parcells after the New Yorkers defeated the Denver Broncos in Super Bowl XXI following the 1986 season. Parcells and the Giants would win it again four years later.

There's little doubt that Jerry Rice is the greatest pass receiver ever. Playing most of his career with the San Francisco 49ers, Rice holds virtually all the major pass receiving records and continued to be a productive player as he neared the age of 40.

While both the Giants and Bears remained formidable teams, the decade ended with San Francisco reestablishing itself and Joe Montana as football's best and as the team of the 1980s. The 'Niners were just 10-6 in the regular season, while the Bears were 12-4. Yet when the two teams met for the NFC title, San Francisco won easily, 28-3, as Joe Montana had a new favorite receiver in wideout Jerry Rice.

In the Super Bowl, the 'Niners showed their toughness by coming from behind to defeat the Cincinnati Bengals 20-16. To do it, San Francisco had to score fourteen fourth-quarter points to erase a 13-6 deficit. Montana completed twenty-three of thirty-six passes for 357 yards, and Rice caught eleven for 215 yards. Together, the pair had become a devastating

RICE IS NICE

Jerry Rice was born on October 13, 1962, in Crawford, Mississippi. After attending Mississippi Valley State College, Rice was drafted by the 49ers prior to the 1985 season, just after the 'Niners had won their second Super Bowl. The 6'2", 200-pound wide receiver immediately began showing his special talents, catching forty-nine passes for 927 yards. A year later he grabbed eighty-six for 1,570 yards and fifteen touchdowns, and the year after that he was on the receiving end of twenty-two scoring aerials.

Rice was a real weapon, a player who could catch the ball over the middle, by the sideline, or deep downfield. After making the grab he was even more dangerous because of his tremendous speed and running ability. It wouldn't be long before he was called one of the greatest ever, and finally the greatest ever. Jerry Rice was still playing as of 2005 and already held all the major pass receiving records. Through 2004, he had caught 1,549 passes for 22,895 yards and 197 TD tosses, all NFL records.

comb nation. A year later, under new coach George Siefert, the 'Niners went 14-2 and easily defeated the Vikings and the Rams to return to the Super Bowl once more. This time they completely blasted Denver, 55-10, with Montana completing twenty-two of twenty-nine passes for 297 yards and Rice grabbing seven for 148 yards. Montana also threw for five touchdowns, three of them to Jerry Rice, and with their fourth Super Bowl victory the San Francisco 49ers definitely earned the label as the team of the 1980s.

Late-Eighties Developments

Professional football continued to grow and develop in the late 1980s. More outstanding players—such as Joe Montana, Jerry Rice, Walter Payton, Dan Marino, and John Elway—began staking their claims to greatness, and the league made some other moves, as well. Let's look at a few:

• Walter Payton retired at the end of the 1987 season as the NFL's all-time leading rusher with 16,726 yards. He rarely missed a game, once playing 186 in a row. Sadly, he died in 1999 at the age of forty-five.

• Though the Miami Dolphins did not return to the Super Bowl after the 1984 season, Dan Marino continued his march to becoming the most prolific passing quarterback of all time.

• In 1983, NFL owners voted to continue an instant replay system to check questionable calls by allowing the referee to view videotapes right on the sideline. It is now a staple of the game.

• The Cardinals franchise was transferred from St. Louis to Phoenix, Arizona.

• Super Bowl XXIII, in which San Francisco defeated Cincinnati 20-16, was watched by more than 110 million viewers, making it the sixth-most-watched

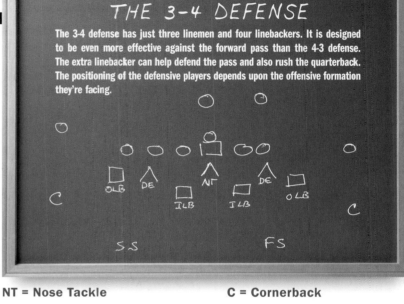

NT = Nose Tackle

OLB = Outside Linebacker

ILB = Inside Linebacker

C = Cornerback

SS = Strong Safety

FS = Free Safety

program in television history. The game was also seen live or on tape in sixty foreign countries, including an estimated 300 million new fans in China.

• Paul Tagliabue was named the seventh commissioner in NFL history, replacing the retired Pete Rozelle.

As the NFL entered the 1990s, the sport would change even more. Free agency and salary cap constraints would increase player movement and make it more difficult for good teams to stay together year after year. This ultimately led to more equality among teams, so it would become increasingly difficult for a team to dominate an era, as the Packers, Steelers, and 49ers had done. But it was still football and still played by the best players in the world, a colorful, action-packed sport that, after seventy years, was still continuing to grow.

New stars always continue to come. Here Dallas Cowboys quarterback Troy Aikman gets set to pass in a 1994 game against the Arizona Cardinals. Aikman came out of UCLA to lead the Cowboys to a trio of Super Bowl wins.

CHAPTER 8

Pro Football—America's Game

There was little doubt at the outset of the 1990s that NFL football had become an American ritual, a great spectator sport that generated excitement all over the country. The Super Bowl had become an event that transcended the sport, a highly anticipated prime-time program that even the casual and non-fan wouldn't miss. And on the field, the game continued to change and evolve, as old stars left and new ones rose to prominence.

In a much more media-driven climate there was more focus on the individual stars of the game than ever before. During the first half of this era, 1990–1997, some older franchises dominated the game. For the second half, 1998–2005, the patterns changed with some new entries at the top of the heap, as well as a couple of old teams in new cities. And finally, the near impossible happened. In an age when people didn't think a single team could be dominant, the New England Patriots shocked the football world by winning the Super Bowl three times in four seasons.

In 1990, the Giants, Bears, and 49ers took the division titles in the NFC, teams that had been at or near the top for years. In the AFC, it was the Buffalo Bills, Cincinnati Bengals, and Los Angeles Raiders. Once again, the Giants had the best defense in the league, yielding just 211 points. But the highest-scoring team was in the AFC, the Buffalo Bills, and many thought Marv Levy's squad was the NFL's best. The NFC had won the last six Super Bowls, so AFC fans were hopeful.

The Bills' explosive offense keyed off quarterback Jim Kelly and running back Thurman Thomas, who led the AFC in passing and running, respectively. James Lofton and Andre Reed were the top pass receivers. The defense was led by a terrific pass rusher in Bruce Smith, as well as linebackers Cornelius Bennett and Darryl Talley.

This was a strong, well-rounded team, and in the AFC title game they destroyed the Raiders, 51-3.

As for the Giants, Bill Parcells' team had many holdovers from the 1986 title group, including quarterback Phil Simms, tight end Mark Bavaro, defensive end Leonard Marshall, linebacker Carl Banks, and, most notably, the awesome Lawrence Taylor. In the NFC title game the Giants just squeezed by the San Francisco 49ers, 15-13, and many wondered if they could handle the Bills. Six of the last seven Super Bowls were blowouts or close to blowouts, and many fans wondered when they would get another hotly contested game. They were about to find out.

With Phil Simms injured, the Giants had to depend on second-string quarterback Jeff Hostetler, but the team felt he could do the job. Yet when the Bills jumped out to a 12-3 lead midway through the second period, it looked as if they were taking charge. But Hostetler brought the Giants back and completed a 14-yard scoring pass to Stephen Baker that brought the score to 12-10 at the half. By then, Coach Parcells saw that even his great defense was having problems containing the Buffalo offense. He decided his team would have its best chance to win if it controlled the football and kept it out of Jim Kelly's hands.

The Giants took the second-half kickoff and embarked on a 75-yard scoring drive that took fourteen plays and consumed a Super Bowl record of nine minutes and twenty-nine seconds. It ended when Ottis Anderson ran the ball over the goal line from the one-yard line. The score gave the Giants a 17-12 lead. At the end of the third quarter Buffalo starting driving again, and on the first play of the final session Thurman Thomas broke loose and ran thirty-one yards for a touchdown. The kick made it 19-17, Bills.

Again the Giants controlled the ball and moved it upfield. Another long drive ended with a 21-yard Matt Bahr field goal, putting New York in front 20-19. It finally came down to the last play of the game. Buffalo had the ball, and Scott Norwood prepared to try a 47-yard field goal for the win. He booted it far enough, but at the last second, it sailed just wide right. The Giants had won their second Super Bowl by a single point, and the NFL had the nail-biter it wanted. It was a tense game in which the Giants held the ball for forty minutes and thirty-three seconds. In the second half, the Bills' offense had the ball for less than eight minutes. Parcells' strategy had worked.

After Washington emerged the next year to whip Buffalo in Super Bowl XXVI, 37-24, an old power reemerged with a new coach and revamped team. The Dallas Cowboys, so successful from the late 1960s right through the mid-1980s, had finally bottomed out. Tom Landry had been the Cowboys' only coach since they were born to expansion in 1960. The team began losing in 1986 and by 1988 finished last at 3-13. That's when the team was sold and the new owner, Jerry Jones, decided he wanted a new coach. That man was Jimmy Johnson, a successful college coach at the University of Miami.

Emmitt Smith has plenty to be happy about. Not only did he play on those great Dallas Cowboys Super Bowl teams, but the relentless halfback has now gained more yards than any player in NFL history.

The team was 1-15 in Johnson's first year of 1989. But he had drafted a big, 6'4", 215-pound quarterback named Troy Aikman out of UCLA. They also had a young wide receiver in Michael Irvin and would soon draft a tenacious running back named Emmitt Smith. This trio would key a great offense. At the same time, Johnson built a formidable defense, and the result was a 13-3 season in 1992 and a 12-4 record the next year. From there, the Cowboys dominated the playoffs and went on to win two straight Super Bowls, 52-17 and 30-13. Their victims both times were the Buffalo Bills.

The league also continued to grow. In 1993, the Carolina Panthers and Jacksonville Jaguars became the NFL's twenty-ninth and thirtieth franchises, set to begin play in 1994. And that same season another familiar group of faces returned to the top. The San Francisco 49ers had the NFL's best record of 13-3 in 1994, scoring 505 points with an explosive offense. The difference was that the quarterback was not Joe Montana but southpaw thrower Steve Young.

Young was a 6'2", 200-pounder out of Brigham Young University. His first stop after college was the upstart United States Football

Detroit halfback Barry Sanders was an incredible broken-field runner who could change direction on a dime. He had the misfortune to play with mostly mediocre Detroit teams but was a record-setting performer and one of the best ever.

A RUNNING BACK NAMED BARRY

When Barry Sanders joined the Detroit Lions out of Oklahoma State in 1989, most people thought he would be good. But few knew he would be that good! Just 5'8" and 203 pounds, Sanders didn't appear to be a typical NFL running back. But he was fast and shifty, could change direction in a split second, and gave defenders fits. He ran low to ground, making him difficult to tackle, and he was rarely caught from behind. He gained 1,470 yards on 280 carries as a rookie, averaging 5.3 yards a pop, and that was just the beginning.

In fact, he would gain more than 1,000 yards in each of his ten seasons, including an amazing 2,053 yards in 1997, a year in which he averaged 6.1 yards a carry. The problem was that the Lions usually had mediocre teams during Sanders' tenure, and he was rarely in the playoffs. At the end of the 1998 season, Sanders had gained 15,269 yards in just ten seasons. He was just thirty years old and seemed a cinch to break Walter Payton's all-time rushing record when he abruptly announced his retirement. Barry Sanders just walked away at the top of his game and never returned. Atlanta defensive back D.J. Johnson summed up Barry Sanders' ability when he said, "He makes you miss so bad, you kind of look up in the stands and wonder if anybody's looking at you."

League in 1984. He then spent two years with the NFL Tampa Bay Buccaneers before being traded to the 49ers in 1987. The problem was he couldn't crack the lineup because the already-legendary Joe Montana was still the number-one quarterback.

By 1991, the 'Niners decided to make a change. Montana moved on to Kansas City, and Young was given the starting job. He quickly showed he was more than up to it, becoming the NFL's Most Valuable Player in 1992 and again in 1994. Young was an accurate thrower and a much better runner than Montana, but there was one knock. Montana had led the 'Niners to four Super Bowl triumphs and Young had none. Finally, in 1994 that all changed. In the regular season, Young led the NFC in passing for the fourth consecutive year, completing 324 of 461 for 3,969 yards with thirty-five touchdowns and just ten interceptions. His quarterback ranking of 112.8 broke Montana's record 112.4, set in 1989.

This was San Francisco's year. The 'Niners first whipped the Bears 44-15 in the divisional playoff, then ended the Dallas Cowboys' two-year reign with a 38-28 win in the NFC title game. Finally, Young and his teammates put on an impressive display in topping the San Diego Chargers, 49-26, in Super Bowl XXIX. Not only did the win make the 'Niners the first team ever to win five Super Bowls, but Steve Young's record-setting, six-touchdown performance firmly established him as one of the game's finest quarterbacks.

More Outstanding Players

A look at the leaders in most offensive categories in the first half of 1990 reflects a changing of the guard. The top passers were Jim Kelly of Buffalo, Warren Moon of Houston, John Elway of Denver, Steve Young of San Francisco, Brett Favre of Green Bay, and great veteran Dan Marino in Miami. Top rushers included Barry Sanders of Detroit, Thurman Thomas of Buffalo, Emmitt Smith of Dallas, Chris Warren of Seattle, and Curtis Martin of New England, while the top pass receivers included Haywood Jefferies of Houston, Michael Irvin of Dallas, Sterling Sharpe of Green Bay, Cris Carter of Minnesota, Herman Moore of Detroit, and still Jerry Rice of the 49ers.

THE LINEMEN TAKE A BOW

Big, bad defensive tackle Howie Long may be known for his TV work today, but he was a perennial All-Pro with the Raiders and one of the best of the 1990s.

A few of the outstanding linemen have been cited in this book, but not enough of them. As mentioned earlier, there was more identification with defensive lines in the 1960s and 1970s because they stayed together for so long. That gradually disappeared in the 1980s and 1990s. Looking at the NFL teams of the 1980s and 1990s, here are some of the great linemen who dominated at their position.

In the 1980s, offensive linemen Anthony Munoz, Gary Zimmerman, Joe Jacoby, John Hannah, Russ Grimm, Dwight Stephenson, and Mike Webster were consistently considered the best. Defensive linemen starring in the 1980s were Reggie White, Howie Long, Lee Roy Selmon, Bruce Smith, Randy White, Dan Hampton, Keith Millard, and Dave Butz. Top offensive linemen of the 1990s include Tony Boselli, Larry Allen, Randall McDaniel, William Roaf, and Mark Stepnoski. Defensive linemen (not already mentioned in the 1980s group) include Chris Doleman, Neil Smith, Cortez Kennedy, John Randle, Warren Sapp, and Bryant Young.

They may not be household names, but these men often had as much to do with the success of their teams as players from other positions.

Some records began to fall during this period. Cris Carter caught a new high of 122 passes in 1994, and a year later Herman Moore broke it by catching 123. But further evidence of the shorter and safer passing game, i.e., the West Coast Offense, can be seen by the average yards per catch. Back in 1939, Don Hutson led the league with just thirty-four catches, but he averaged 24.9 yards a catch. In 1951, Elroy "Crazylegs" Hirsch led with sixty-six grabs and averaged 22.7 yards per grab. The highest average per catch from a league leader between 1990 and 2004 was 16.4 yards by Irvin in 1991. There were many more passes being thrown, but most were of the short and medium-range variety. The long bomb, once one of the game's most electrifying plays, was often relegated to last-second, desperation situations. There were no Joe Namaths throwing long to Don Maynard, or Daryle Lamonicas airing it out to Warren Wells or Cliff Branch.

Linemen were also becoming larger during this period. When the Redskins won the Super Bowl following the 1991 season, their offensive line was dubbed the "Hawgs," because of their girth. Refrigerator Perry made a big splash in 1985 because of his 300-pound-plus weight. But now more and more 300-pound linemen were coming into the league, and many of them were fast and agile.

Linemen are often the unsung heroes of the game. A team cannot win without a strong offensive and defensive line. The offensive line must block efficiently on runs and protect the quarterback on pass plays. Defensive linemen must be able to put pressure on the passer and stop the running game at the line of scrimmage. Defensive ends, especially, should be good pass rushers and fast enough to chase running plays to the outside. For years, linemen didn't make the same kind of money as quarterbacks, running backs, wide receivers, and even some linebackers. Today, the top offensive and defensive linemen also make the big bucks. And they earn it.

An Old Champ Returns and New Champs Rise

Following the 1995 season, Dallas won its third Super Bowl title in four years, this time whipping the Pittsburgh Steelers 27-17. The victory enabled the Cowboys to tie the 49ers with five Super Bowl titles. But it would be their last, so far. The next season, an old power rose up again in the frozen North. The Green Bay Packers, led by a tough, gutsy, gambling quarterback named Brett Favre, would be the NFL's best team in 1996.

Favre was drafted by the Atlanta Falcons out of Southern Mississippi in 1991. It seemed a perfect fit, a Southern-born quarterback who stayed at home to play at Southern Miss now going to a Southern team. But the Falcons used him in just two games his rookie year, then decided he didn't fit. They traded him to the Green Bay Packers, where he quickly claimed the starting job in 1992. Not only did he emerge as a starter, but the kid from the South seemed to thrive in the frozen North, especially in December games played on the "frozen tundra" of Green Bay.

By 1995, Favre was the NFC's leading passer, completing 359 of 570 passes for 4,413 yards and thirty-eight touchdowns. He was intercepted just thirteen times. There was little doubt that Favre was already a star. A year later, he led the Packers to a 13-3 record and finally a 35-21 Super Bowl victory over New England. It was the Packers' first Super Bowl win since the Lombardi era, when they won the first two ever played, and Brett Favre was the toast of the town.

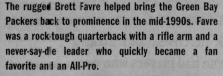

The rugged Brett Favre helped bring the Green Bay Packers back to prominence in the mid-1990s. Favre was a rock-tough quarterback with a rifle arm and a never-say-die leader who quickly became a fan favorite and an All-Pro.

Favre continues to be one of the NFL's all-time best and one of its toughest players. He always plays all-out, yet as of 2005, hadn't missed a start in thirteen years. He brought the Pack back to the Super Bowl after the 1997 season, though they were beaten that year by the Denver Broncos. Yet Brett Favre has cemented his reputation as a never-say-die player who is a threat to lead his team to victory right up until the final gun.

While Brett Favre made his reputation early in his career, another great quarterback confirmed his legacy late. John Elway was drafted out of Stanford University, where he starred in both baseball and football, and set several NCAA passing records. The problem was he was drafted by the Baltimore Colts in 1983 and said he wouldn't play there. The Colts didn't want a disgruntled player, so they traded him to the Denver Broncos for two players and a first-round draft choice.

Elway was a strong-armed quarterback who was criticized early for trying to force throws into tight coverage because of the confidence he had in his throwing arm. But he also showed a capacity for bringing his team from behind with clutch, last-minute drives, something he would do throughout his career. By 1986, Elway helped the Broncos get to the Super Bowl, but the Giants beat them, 39-20, in Super Bowl XXI. The next year they were back, and the

Strong-armed John Elway played in an era of great quarterbacks and was one of the best. He specialized in last-second comebacks and in the twilight of his career led the Denver Broncos to a pair of Super Bowl championships.

Redskins beat them 42-10. Two years after that, Elway had them in the big game again, and this time they were crushed by the 49ers, 55-10. As terrific as Elway was, people said he couldn't win the big one.

It took another eight years, but finally in 1997 the Broncos rose to the top of the heap. With the help of running back Terrell Davis, who gained 1,750 yards, the Broncos rode into the playoffs and wound up defeating the Green Bay Packers 31-24. A year later they did it again, this time whipping the surprising Atlanta Falcons 34-19. Elway had come full cycle, finishing his career with a pair of Super Bowl rings as trophies, and he retired on top.

The outstanding running backs just keep coming, even in an era when the forward pass dominates offenses. Despite the presence of an outstanding quarterback like a Brett Favre or John Elway, it still helps to have a reliable 1,000-yard runner, a workhorse who can carry the ball twenty-five times a game. Emmitt Smith did the job for the Dallas Cowboys and would eventually pass Walter Payton as the NFL's all-time leading rusher. Smith was steady, if not spectacular. But throughout the 1990s and into the twenty-first century, a whole new group of running backs excelled.

Terrell Davis won three straight AFC rushing titles, topping it off with a 2,008-yard season in 1998. Jamal Anderson of Atlanta had 1,846 yards that same year, setting a record with 410 carries. Ironically, both those players had their careers shortened by knee injuries. There were other great performances as well. Edgerin James of the Indianapolis Colts gained 1,709 yards in 2000. Priest Holmes of the Chiefs ran for 1,555 yards in 2001. Ricky Williams of the Dolphins gained 1,853 yards in 2002, and a year later, Ahman Green of the Packers had 1,883 yards, while Jamal Lewis of the Baltimore Ravens gained 2,066. In 2004, Curtis Martin, now with the New York Jets, not only led the NFL with 1,697 yards but tied Barry Sanders' record of gaining 1,000 or more yards in each of his first ten seasons.

Running back Curtis Martin

The St. Louis Rams, led by an arena football alumnus at quarterback, Kurt Warner, won Super Bowl XXXV over the Tennessee Titans, 23-16, following the 1999 season. A year later it was the surprising Baltimore Ravens, led by running back Jamal Lewis and middle linebacker Ray Lewis, defeating the New York Giants 34-7 to become champs. Because of free agency and increased player movement, most observers felt that new teams would rise to the top each year. There was doubt that a single team could ever dominate over a period of time again. That's before the New England Patriots under Coach Bill Belichick came along.

The Patriots redefined the team concept. They were a team without a huge star, but they did have a very efficient quarterback in young Tom Brady. If there was a star, however, it had to be the coach. Belichick had been an assistant under Bill Parcells for years. He once coached the Cleveland Browns for several seasons but was eventually fired. Once the Patriots put the team in his hands, he not only built them into a champion but also gained the reputation as the best coach in the game.

The Pats would win three Super Bowls in four years, defeating St. Louis 20-17 in a huge upset in Super Bowl XXXVI. After Tampa Bay won it over Oakland the following year, the Patriots came back to win two more, beating Carolina, 32-29, then Philadelphia, 24-21. Both were close games, but Belichick's teams always seemed to find a way to win. The coach was a master at devising defensive schemes, creating ways for his offense to attack defenses, and making mid-game adjustments. And he made sure he had players who would follow his game plans to the letter. With an outstanding defense and a clutch quarterback who reminds many of Joe Montana, the Patriots have been the most successful team since the Cowboys won three in four years from 1992 to 1995.

In many ways, professional football has come full circle. In 2004, there were thirty-two NFL teams. Both the NFC and AFC had four divisions of four teams each, with the four division winners and two wild card teams from each conference going to the playoffs. That's twelve teams with a shot at winning the championship. Remember, in the earliest days the team with the best record was declared champ. Then there was a title game between the two division winners. After that, there were two title games and the Super Bowl. And after the merger in 1970, it all began to grow.

The Houston Texans and new Cleveland Browns are the latest teams to join the league. The original Browns moved to Baltimore and became the Ravens. That was after the old Baltimore Colts moved to Indianapolis. Then the Texans came to Houston after the Oilers moved to Tennessee and became the Titans. Even the Raiders moved again. After leaving Oakland for Los Angeles in 1982, the team returned to Oakland for the 1995 season. And, of course, the old L.A. Rams are now in St. Louis. So franchise movement has continued.

But the game remains great. New players continue to come, and all records are there to be broken. When quarterback Dan Marino retired following the 2000 season, he held virtually every passing record, throwing for 420 touchdowns, 61,361 yards, and completing 4,967 passes, including forty-eight TDs in a single season. The one blot on his record was that his team never won a Super Bowl.

In 2004, Peyton Manning of the Indianapolis Colts broke one of Marino's records by throwing forty-nine TD passes during the season. Manning, the son of former New Orleans quarterback Archie Manning, is now recognized as the best pure passer in the league. And Marvin Harrison, Manning's favorite receiver, set a new record in 2002 when he caught an amazing 143 passes. But like Marino, Manning has yet to lead his team to that final victory, the one that says his team is the world champion.

Manning's Colts finished at 14–2 in 2005 and were the favorites to win the title. But they were upset in the divisional playoffs by the wild card Pittsburgh Steelers, the last team in the AFC to make the playoffs. The Steelers, under Coach Bill Cowher, won three straight playoff games on the road and then defeated the Seattle Seahawks, 21–10, in Super Bowl XL to become champions, their first title in 26 years and fifth overall.

A Long History Continues

There it is, fans, more than one hundred years of football. I've tried to touch on all the highlights, the events and players who have shaped and changed the game, as well as the moments that will always be remembered. Along the way you've seen how the National Football League was started, grew, expanded, and became part of American life. You've learned about the record-setting players and great championship games that can still be seen via films and tapes. So the history of the NFL is still alive for everyone to enjoy.

When all is said and done, winning remains the goal of every team and every player who puts on cleats, pads, and helmet and runs onto the gridiron to play the game he loves. Professional football is a difficult game played by tough men who have to work very hard to excel, no matter what position they play. But then again, it has always been that way, and every player from Jim Thorpe to Peyton Manning never wanted it to be any different. They all love the individual challenge, the competition, being part of a team, and working together for the same goal—to be a champion in the National Football League.

Peyton Manning (18) is from a quarterback family. Dad Archie played for the New Orleans Saints in the seventies, and brother Eli is with the New York Giants.

American Football League (AFL): Most recently, a professional league of American football existing from 1960 to 1969 that merged with the National Football League in 1970.

Blitz: A run made by linebackers and defensive backs in an effort to sack the quarterback before he can hand off the ball or make a pass.

Center: an offensive line position at the center of the line of scrimmage. The center snaps the ball to the quarterback or punter.

Coin toss: To decide which team kicks off, the visiting captain calls "heads" or "tails" of a coin flipped by the referee.

Conversion: the scoring of an additional point or two points after a touchdown.

Cornerback: a defensive player whose role is to tackle runners and defend against or intercept passes.

Defense: the team defending their goal line; also the team attempting to prevent the offense from passing or running the ball over their goal line.

Defensive linemen: the players whose role is to tackle running backs and to prevent the quarterback from completing a pass that gains yards.

Down: an offensive play that begins when the center snaps the ball to the quarterback, to be passed or run to gain yards, and ends when the referee blows the whistle to indicate the play is over.

End: one of two offensive linemen on the end of the line of scrimmage who block defensive linemen, catch passes, and sometimes guard the quarterback. In today's professional game, the tight end lines up at the end of the line but the split end is usually 10 yards or so away from the line.

End zone: a 10-yard-deep area at either end of the field between the goal line and the end line.

Field goal: a placekick successfully through the goalpost that is worth three points.

Formation: generally, the strategic arrangement of both defensive and offensive players at the beginning of a play.

Fullback: an offensive player whose role it is to block for the halfback and the quarterback, run the ball, and receive passes.

Fumble: a ball that is dropped while in play.

Guard: one of two offensive linemen, on either side of the center, designated to guard the quarterback and block for running backs.

Halfback: (also known as *tailback* or *running back*) an offensive player whose role it is to run the ball, receive passes, and block for any teammate in possession of the ball.

Hash marks: marks that divide the field into thirds.

Huddle: the gathering of players in a circle or semi-circle to plan the next play. On offense, it is the quarterback who gives the instructions. On defense, it is usually a linebacker.

Incomplete: a forward pass that is not caught or intercepted.

Kickoff: a free kick, from the 35-yard line, by the winner of the coin toss that begins the game or after a touchdown is scored.

Lateral: a forward pass that is thrown in any direction other than toward the opponent's goal line.

Linebacker: one of three or four defensive players, placed behind the defensive linemen, whose role it is to tackle runners, rush the quarterback, or to block or intercept passes.

Line of scrimmage: an imaginary line parallel to the goal lines and at the most forward point of the football when it is on the ground in position to be put in play at the beginning of each down.

Man in motion: the offensive player who runs behind, but parallel to, the line of scrimmage before the ball is snapped.

Offense: the team in possession of the ball, trying to advance it toward the opponent's goal line by running or passing.

Offensive linemen: seven players: the center, two guards, two ends, and two tackles.

Official: someone who directs the game by making sure the rules are followed and calls penalties when they are broken.

Offsides: when a player crosses the opposing team's side (line of scrimmage) before the ball is snapped.

Pass rush: the rush by the defense to tackle the quarterback before he can complete a pass.

Pocket: the area a few yards behind the line of scrimmage for which protection is created by blockers and from which the quarterback passes.

Punt: play during which the ball is dropped from the kicker's hands and kicked before it hits the ground.

Quarterback: the offensive player responsible for taking the snap, handing it to a running back, or passing it to gain yards toward the opposition's goal line. Occasionally, the quarterback will also run the ball.

Receiver: the offensive member whose role it is to catch a pass from the quarterback and to run it downfield.

Running back: an offensive player whose primary responsibility is running with the ball, but he can block and catch passes as well.

Rush: to run from the line of scrimmage with the ball.

Sack: to tackle the quarterback behind the line of scrimmage before he can pass the ball.

Safety: two points awarded the defensive team when a member of the offensive team is tackled behind the goal line in his own end zone.

Snap: when the center hands the ball off between his legs to the quarterback or punter to begin a down.

Tackle: the act or instance or method of tackling an opponent to stop him from advancing the ball.

Touchdown: the six points received when the offense crosses the goal line either carrying or catching the ball.

Wide receiver: the offensive end located on the far left or right of the offensive line.

FURTHER READING & WEBSITES

Fleder, Rob. *Sports Illustrated: The Football Book.* New York: Sports Illustrated Books, 2005.

Lombardi, Vince. *The Lombardi Rules: 26 Lessons from Vince Lombardi, the World's Greatest Coach.* New York: McGraw-Hill, 2004.

Long, Howie, and John Czarnecki. *Football for Dummies.* Indianapolis: Wiley Publishing, Inc., 1998.

Madden, John, and Dave Anderson. *All Madden: Boom! Bam! Boink!* New York: Harper Collins, 1996.

Polzer, Tim. NFL: *Play Football!* New York: Dorling Kindersley, 2002.

Sports Illustrated 2005 NFL Record and Fact Book. New York: Time Inc. Home Entertainment, 2005.

Whittingham, Richard. *For The Glory of Their Game: Stories of Life in the NFL by the Men Who Lived It.* Chicago: Triumph Books, 2005.

National Football League
www.nfl.com

The official NFL site for kids
www.playfootball.com

The official site of NFL players
www.nflplayers.com

Pro Football Hall of Fame
www.profootballhof.com

Kids Online NFL Football Quiz
www.kidzworld.com/site/p2754.htm